JAN – – 2015

179.3 BOHANEC
Bohanec, Hope.
The ultimate betrayal :is there happy
 meat? / WITHDRAWN

W9-AUM-503

The Ultimate Betrayal

JAN - - 2015

Praise for *The Ultimate Betrayal: Is There Happy Meat?*

The Ultimate Betrayal is a well-rounded and thoroughly-researched book that touches the heart with an honest and unflinching look at the reality behind "humane" labels and processes. With real-life examples from multiple viewpoints and thought-provoking philosophical underpinnings, *The Ultimate Betrayal* is a must-read for anyone interested in ethical food choices.

—Dawn Moncrief, founder, A Well-Fed World

The Ultimate Betrayal is a powerful and insightful text that should be required reading for anyone concerned with animals, humans, or the environment. Despite its growing popularity, "humane slaughter" of animals is an impossibility and this text helps to bring this reality to light. I cannot recommend this book highly enough.

—Vasile Stanescu, co-senior editor, Critical Animal Studies Book Series, Stanford University; associate editor, *Journal for Critical Animals Studies*; instructor, Program in Writing and Rhetoric, Stanford University

The Ultimate Betrayal is sure to be an eye-opener for consumers whose concern for animals leads them to purchase organic or locally raised meat, cage-free eggs, and similar products. This book is a fascinating and in-depth look at what such labels really mean, and whether a kinder choice is possible. Consumers deserve to know the truth.

—Nick Cooney, author, *Change of Heart: What Psychology Can Teach Us about Spreading Social Change*

The Ultimate Betrayal greatly increases awareness that a major societal shift to plant-based diets is essential if we are to have a chance to avert a climate catastrophe; severe food, water and energy scarcities; and other environmental disasters. Especially valuable is the exposing of the myths about the alleged value of alternate means of raising farm animals to reduce animal suffering, improve human health, reduce climate change and other negative environmental impacts. I sincerely hope that this extremely well-researched, well-documented, and well-written book will be widely read and heeded as an important step in shifting our imperiled planet to a sustainable path.

—Richard H. Schwartz, author, *Judaism and Vegetarianism,*
Judaism and Global Survival, Mathematics and Global Survival,
and *Who Stole My Religion?*; president,
Jewish Vegetarians of North America; president,
Society of Ethical and Religious Vegetarians (SERV)

The unspeakable cruelty that farmed animals endure is passionately voiced in *The Ultimate Betrayal,* inspiring us to make more compassionate choices for ourselves, our families, the planet, and the animals. This book shines a spotlight on the false impression of "humane animal products" that was once hiding in the shadows. A must-read for anyone who cares about animals.

—*Cindy Machado, director of Animal Services,*
Marin Humane Society

The Ultimate Betrayal is a timely, thorough, and essential book that exposes the dark side of the "happy meat" movement. With both passion and precision, this book documents the egregious cruelty meted out to cows on organic dairies, hens in free-range egg operations, and pigs on small-scale family farms and sheds much-needed light on both the actual practices as well as the inherent ethical conflicts involved. This book is essential for all of us wishing to understand our culture, our health, and the inescapable repercussions of our mistreatment of animals.

—Dr. Will Tuttle, author of the best-selling *The World Peace Diet* and recipient of the Courage of Conscience Award

The Ultimate Betrayal makes an airtight argument in favor of the individual worth of every animal, irrelevant to their supposed economic value to humans. If there was ever a time to combat the myth of humane animal products, that time is now.

—Michael A. Weber, executive director, Farm Animal Rights Movement (FARM)

Today we are witnessing a significant disconnect between what we choose to eat and the impact those choices have on other living beings, our planet, and ourselves. *The Ultimate Betrayal* provides a compelling view of the magnitude of this disconnect, while inspiring the awareness necessary to effect positive change. I consider it a must-read for anyone who cares about the future of the Earth and its inhabitants.

—Dr. Richard Oppenlander, author of award-winning *Comfortably Unaware*

If you assume that as long as animals are treated humanely it is all right to kill them, *The Ultimate Betrayal* will lead you to question this assumption, and to interrogate more deeply what "humane" really means.

– Karen Davis, PhD, president, United Poultry Concerns

The Ultimate Betrayal thoroughly addresses the oxymoron of humane meat. This book eloquently makes the case that regardless if the pig is raised in a crate or outside, her life still ends inside a slaughterhouse at six months of age. If you are purchasing free-range eggs or "humane" meat, this book is not to be missed!

—Kim Sturla, executive director, Animal Place

A comprehensive and critical study of small-scale animal agriculture that leaves the reader yearning for a truly compassionate way of eating: one that leaves animals off our plates entirely.

—Colleen Patrick-Goudreau, best-selling author and creator of *The 30-Day Vegan Challenge*

The Ultimate Betrayal provides us with a much-needed critical look into the so-called sustainable and humane alternatives to the industrial production of animal products. Combining comprehensive research and engaging prose, this book reminds "conscientious carnivores" that eating animals comes with a realm of unresolved ethical implications. Enlightening us to these implications pushes the world ever closer to a plant-based diet. It's a superb accomplishment.

—James McWilliams, author of *Just Food*

The Ultimate Betrayal

Is There Happy Meat?

Hope Bohanec

with Cogen Bohanec

iUniverse LLC
Bloomington

Alameda Free Library
1550 Oak Street
Alameda, CA 94501

THE ULTIMATE BETRAYAL
IS THERE HAPPY MEAT?

Copyright © 2013 Hope Bohanec.

All rights reserved. No part of this book may be used or reproduced by any means, graphic, electronic, or mechanical, including photocopying, recording, taping or by any information storage retrieval system without the written permission of the publisher except in the case of brief quotations embodied in critical articles and reviews.

iUniverse books may be ordered through booksellers or by contacting:

iUniverse LLC
1663 Liberty Drive
Bloomington, IN 47403
www.iuniverse.com
1-800-Authors (1-800-288-4677)

Because of the dynamic nature of the Internet, any web addresses or links contained in this book may have changed since publication and may no longer be valid. The views expressed in this work are solely those of the author and do not necessarily reflect the views of the publisher, and the publisher hereby disclaims any responsibility for them.

Any people depicted in stock imagery provided by Thinkstock are models, and such images are being used for illustrative purposes only.

Certain stock imagery © Thinkstock.

ISBN: 978-1-4759-9093-5 (sc)
ISBN: 978-1-4759-9094-2 (ebk)

Library of Congress Control Number: 2013910805

Printed in the United States of America

iUniverse rev. date: 08/08/2013

For Brad Larsen whose radiant soul and resplendent smile left us much too soon. Thank you for your endless compassion for all beings and your inspiring optimism; you will be missed.

Contents

Preface

I sat eighty feet above the earth in a precarious, hand-made rope hammock tied between four gigantic redwood trees. Every time I shifted, branches bobbed and the ropes swayed like an uncertain boat in undulating waves. The cold was so biting I don't think I felt my finger tips for all the weeks that I resided in that arboreal wonderland. My body ached from being unable to stand up. There was no one to keep me company except the loggers, who greeted me with their thunderous chainsaws at 4 a.m. My love of nature and animals had taken me outside the mainstream of society and had led me deep into the Northwestern Sequoia forests, where a band of young, dedicated people perilously fought to save the last of the tallest trees on Earth.

The activism of my youth was a mix of exhilaration, heartbreak, and sometimes danger, risking my own safety to help animals and ecosystems. I saw direct action and risky tactics as recompense for being alive. My love for animals and wild places was not a product of socialization, or exposure at a young age, but seemed to come from somewhere deep inside of me. Fresh out of high school, I knew that I had a calling. My first job was with the environmental organization, Greenpeace. I learned about deforestation, how pollutants were poisoning our environment—and what would prove to be most formative for me—I became aware of the devastating impact of animal agriculture.

Eating is such an intimate experience—critical to our lives and well-being. But what we choose to eat has far reaching global impact as well. Once I became aware of the dire consequences of our human eating habits, I turned my attention towards food related issues, particularly animal agriculture. As I learned more, the plight of farmed animals grew closer to my heart. They were the most abused, neglected, and mistreated of all animals in human care, and perhaps among the most anguished beings on the planet. After agonizing over countless hours of documented evidence of the abhorrent conditions in the livestock industry, what I witnessed haunts my soul and has impelled me to dedicate my life to telling these animals' story.

For more than twenty years, I have organized countless events including public education campaigns, demonstrations, and fundraisers to offer a voice for these animals. I was the Sonoma County coordinator for a statewide proposition to help protect farm animals from intensive confinement and co-founded an organization dedicated to supporting cruelty-free food choices. I have rescued starving chickens from windowless warehouses, appeared on national television to debate the benefits of reducing meat consumption, and was the campaigns director at an international animal protection organization.

I wrote this book because the conversation over the last twenty years about our food choices is gradually shifting. I hear people say that they eat "free-range eggs" or "organic meat" and they feel that by doing so, the conversation about animal cruelty has ended. They are now doing what they believe is the right thing to do and that the animals are now "happy." While I am extremely grateful that people are beginning to care about the plight of farmed animals, and willing to seek out these products, we must ask if all the problems are in fact solved with these new labels. Is this really the end of the story? I have conducted extensive research into the issue of alternative animal agricultural methods, interviewed former farm and slaughterhouse workers, and visited farmed animal sanctuaries in search of the truth behind the labels. This book is a reflection on those findings, and it is far from the end of the story.

When my husband, Cogen, and I connected thirteen years ago, I knew that he was the only person I had ever met who truly understood all of me—my compassion for the Earth and her animals, and my aching desire to help them. He understood that this need was more important to me than anything else and has been at my side, offering a supportive but critical role for over a decade. His involvement with, and contributions to this book have been invaluable. He compliments my work with an academic eye and cogent argumentation, making the book more powerful and compelling, and I am forever grateful.

My activism has shifted over the years from fist in the air to fingers on the keyboard as I hope to reach a wider audience with a softer voice. I have faith that our collective circle of compassion will someday widen to include *all* animals. We can and we must learn to live in a way that will benefit the planet and respect other species if our own is to survive. This book represents the accumulation of the knowledge that I have gathered on my journey toward a vision of a compassionate, healthy, and thriving planet. It is my gift to anyone ready to discover the truth of our food choices and willing to move our society toward a better world for all.

Hope Bohanec
Sonoma County, CA

Acknowledgments

Deep gratitude to the following people for their contribution:

Marji Beach; Dr. Holly Cheever; Nick Cooney; Karen Davis, PhD; Ian Elwood; Galen Hazelhofer; Cheryl Leahy; Cindy Machado; James McWilliams; Dawn Moncrief; Dr. Richard Oppenlander; Colleen Patrick-Goudreau; Sophia Rivers; Lily Rex; Richard Schwartz; Paul Shapiro; Vasile Stanescu; Kim Sturla; Will Tuttle; Michael Weber; Ed Yaffa

For their encouragement:

Mandy Cimino; Angie Grainger; Dr. Melanie Joy; Brad Larsen; Kamal Prasad; Wade Spital; and my three Mom's—Darla, Marda, and Mila

For their inspiration:

Bruce Friedrich; Michael Greger, MD; Scotlund Haisley; Dixie Mahy; Erik Marcus; Erica Meier; Bryan Pease; Matt Rossell; Nathan Runkle; Captain Paul Watson; Steve Wells; Tim Woodward

Introduction

Farm animals feel pleasure and sadness, excitement and resentment, depression, fear, and pain. They are far more aware and intelligent than we ever imagined ... they are individuals in their own right.

—Dr. Jane Goodall, primatologist

In the last two decades, our society has seen a steady awakening of concern for the suffering of nonhuman animals. Dedicated people have worked ardently to expose the shocking reality of animal exploitation at human hands. These courageous people shine a spotlight on the darkest shadows of animal anguish in what are often dangerous circumstances, defying the scorn of industry representatives, social norms, and their own acculturation to expose shocking animal abuse. Photos and videos bring evidence to the public's awareness and confirm horror stories told by former employees of research facilities, entertainment industries, and factory farms. Social media brings the distressing truth to our living rooms, and people are bearing witness to the miserable reality so many animals endure. These images and confessions provide cogent testimony to the confined, barren cages and crates—the standard living conditions for exploited animals across industry lines. The abject deprivation of stimulus and kindness is exposed; the denial of basic access to sunlight, soil, clean air, and water is uncovered; and the heartbreaking separation of families is felt. People are becoming aware of the misery and pain inherent in any system that treats animals as commodities.

As a result of these efforts, millions of people are opening their eyes to the horrid circumstances that animals endure for food production in particular. The conditions and treatment on industrial-scale farms and CAFOs (Concentrated Animal Feeding Operations) have become so shocking that no conscientious person who is exposed to the photos and videos could deem these facilities, or the behavior of abusive workers, acceptable. Farmed animals are deeply dependent on us, and we have taken full advantage of our domination over them, creating a system where they are now tormented ghosts in a heartless food machine. Hidden from public sight, cows, pigs, chickens, turkeys and other beautiful, sentient creatures languish in miserable conditions, shuddering from insensitive hands, and enduring immense suffering.

People are waking up to the realization that there is no difference between a cow, a dog, a pig, a cat, or a bird in terms of emotional capacity and their potential to suffer. Each is an animal with similar needs and life experiences: each hungers, appreciates a kind hand, experiences pain, and attempts to flee from perceived danger—each of them wants to live.

Researchers have consistently discovered that people are uncomfortable with the improper treatment of animals raised in food production.[1, 2] Even a small amount of interaction with a companion animal reveals that each cat, dog, horse, and rabbit is an individual, sensitive to the maladies of hunger and thirst, fear and distress, joy and sorrow. We are finding that there is an inherent discomfort with knowing that someone has, even inadvertently, caused the suffering of an animal, especially one that is eaten.

This development has inspired a shift in the way farmed animals are being raised, labeled, and presented to the consumer. Caring people who don't want to participate in the suffering of animals are seeking alternatives, and the industry is responding. This is an extraordinary step in a compassionate direction. People are acknowledging that farmed animals are living in misery and that their physical and emotional well-being matters. They concede that animals raised for food deserve to live happy lives. Small-scale operations are the latest trend, local is the new black, and various methods of alternative animal farming with feel-good labels are all the rage. It is now fashionable to express that your eggs are free-range and that your meat is organic. A customer wants to be reassured—but is this fad really the answer to the plentiful problems of raising animals for food? What do the labels really mean? Are these new products actually ethical? Environmentally friendly? Sustainable? We will be exploring answers to these critical questions in the following chapters.

Farm Animals Are Emotional and Intelligent Beings

The fact that animals feel pain and suffer has become not only widely accepted but virtually undebatable.[3, 4, 5] Science is exploring how to gauge the extent of animal pain and suffering, as well as how to reduce it, with a variety of applications including farming.[6, 7, 8, 9] But what do we know of animals' emotional lives and consciousness? All mammals and avians, including farmed animals, are sentient beings, capable of thinking for themselves and feeling many of the same emotions that we do: they seek companionship, many are playful, they are curious about the world, and they investigate new things. Scientific studies are increasingly shedding light on the fact that farmed animals have complex social, emotional, and intellectual existences.[10, 11] Recently, an international group of prominent scientists signed a declaration stating that all mammals, birds, and even the octopus are as conscious and aware as humans. Called The Cambridge Declaration on Consciousness, this document emerges after decades of scientific research, with the data overwhelmingly pointing to animals having clear conscious states of awareness.[12] The declaration's signers said, "Convergent evidence indicates that nonhuman animals have the neuroanatomical, neurochemical, and neurophysiological substrates of conscious states along with the capacity to exhibit intentional behaviors. Consequently, the weight of evidence indicates that humans are not unique in possessing the neurological substrates that generate consciousness. Nonhuman animals, including all mammals and birds, and many other creatures, including octopuses, also possess these neurological substrates." Renowned scientists now assert that animals are as conscious and aware as humans.[13] We can no longer say "they are just stupid animals" as science and common sense are proving differently.

When we see a cow peacefully munching grass in a field, her calm demeanor and steady stare may fool us into thinking that there is not a lot going on in that huge head of hers, but that is far from the truth. Marc Bekoff, an ethologist and author of numerous books on animal behavior, has written extensively about the emotional lives of animals and of cows; he writes, "Cows are very intelligent. They worry over what they don't understand and have been shown to experience 'eureka' moments when they solve a puzzle, such as when they figure out how to open a particularly difficult gate."[14]

Cows are very social animals who form strong familial bonds and friendships within their herd. A researcher from Northampton University in England placed cows in different pens to test their stress responses via their heart rate, cortisol (stress hormone) levels, and behavior. Cows were relaxed and at ease, with slow heart rates, when bunking with a friend, but when their buddy was taken away and replaced with a stranger, they showed signs of stress via increased heart rate and higher cortisol levels.[15]

Dr. Holly Cheever, now with the Humane Society Veterinary Medical Association, was a large animal vet for many years. During her practice, she was called out one day to a dairy to try to solve a mystery. A farmer contacted her and said that one of his cows, who had recently given birth to a calf and should be producing milk, was returning to the barn each day with an empty udder. The farmer was stumped as to why she was not giving milk.

Upon arriving, the vet inquired about the cow and found out that she had given birth three times before without incident. Dr. Cheever was also puzzled, as there seemed to be no medical reason for the empty udder. She decided to return in the morning and follow the cow out to the field, as this lucky girl had the rare pleasure of daily access to a grassy pasture. Dr. Cheever followed her all the way to the edge of the grazing land where the grass met a tree line of forest, and there, in a thicket of bush and trees, lay a quiet baby calf awaiting her morning milk. The cow had given birth to twins, and in a heart-wrenching "Sophie's choice," had returned one to the barn, knowing full well that the calf would be taken from her, and then hidden the other, safely tucked in the trees, where she could come and care for her every day.

This remarkable act of compassionate motherhood demonstrates that she had the hindsight to remember that her previous calves had been taken from her at birth. She also knew that bringing back just one would satisfy the farmer, and then she could keep the other for herself, to nurture and love. It took planning, cunning, foresight, and courage—emotions and attributes normally thought only to be possessed by humans.

When people visit farm sanctuaries, they are often surprised that it is chickens who they are drawn to, for their individual personalities and emotional expressions of curiosity and affection. Chickens have better eyesight and hearing than humans, and they see a full spectrum of light, from ultraviolet to infrared. When a rooster crows just before dawn, he is seeing the infrared early-morning light before a human can. Chickens' beaks have sensitive nerve receptors and play a vital role in their experience of the world, being used to forage for food, preen their feathers, gather nesting materials, and defend themselves.

They may appear very different from us, with their jittery, cautious behavior, but studies show that chickens are intelligent beings—they anticipate the future and are capable of understanding cause-and-effect relationships with a wide range of emotions. Contrary to popular belief, chickens outperform dogs and cats in many advanced cognition tests, exposing their innate intelligence. Ethologist Dr. Lesley Rogers notes, "it is now clear that birds have cognitive capacities equivalent to those of mammals, even primates."[16]

In fact, chickens have attributes previously thought only to be found in humans and primates: expectation of the future and self-control. In a study by the Silsoe Research Institute in England, scientists showed that chickens have the ability to make a conscious choice to postpone gratification. In the study, chickens were presented with buttons that, when pressed, produced food. When pressed quickly, the buttons yielded only a small amount of food. The chickens learned, however, that waiting before pressing the button would result in a greater reward. The hens controlled their impulsive inclinations and chose to wait for the bigger payout over ninety percent of the time, proving that chickens have an important aspect of cognition: they can anticipate the future.[17]

One revealing study shows that hens empathize with their chicks, even when they are just mildly distressed. Chicks were exposed to a puff of air every thirty seconds that caused them slight discomfort. Seeing and sensing their babies' distress, the hens' heart rates increased, and their eye moisture decreased (a sign of alertness and stress). Behavior also changed, with increased awareness, decreased preening, and increased vocalizations directed at the chicks. A coauthor of the study stated, "We found that adult female birds possess at least one of the essential underpinning attributes of 'empathy': the ability to be affected by, and share, the emotional state of another."[18]

The emotional and physical capacity for farm animals to suffer is even accepted within the animal livestock industry. In the following statement referring to the aforementioned empathy study on The Poultry Site (a poultry industry website) they readily admit that chickens in animal agriculture frequently suffer. From The Poultry Site, "The researchers used chickens as a model species because, under commercial conditions, chickens will regularly encounter other chickens showing signs of pain or distress due to routine husbandry practices or because of the high levels of conditions such as bone fractures or leg disorders."[19] Through science and observation we are learning that there is much more to chickens than was once believed. With a range of surprising capabilities and emotions, these feathered friends are startlingly like us.

Sheep also display an intelligence that reveals their astonishing emotional complexities. A study found they can remember up to one hundred human faces and are drawn to a smile; sheep will choose to approach a smiling person before a frowning or neutral face.[20] It would appear that not only can they recognize friendliness, but like humans, they prefer it.

Sheep are also able to learn and remember how to navigate complicated mazes[21] and scored outstandingly on a cognitive and intelligence test where they had to adapt to changing circumstances to solve puzzles. The researchers were surprised at the exceptional cognitive abilities of the sheep and said, "Sheep can perform 'executive' cognitive tasks that are an important part of the primate behavioral repertoire but that have never been shown previously to exist in any other large animal" other than humans and some other primates.[22] Sheep in Yorkshire, England have learned to roll themselves over cattle grates to access tasty village gardens and fields. A witness observed, "They lie down on their side, and just roll over and over the grates until they are clear."[23] The National Sheep Association states, "Sheep are quite intelligent creatures and have more brainpower than people are willing to give them credit for."

Pigs on the other hand, are sometimes recognized for their intelligence. One study found that pigs, with joystick in snout, played video games with more concentration and precision than chimpanzees.[24] More recent studies have found that pigs are also self-aware. Scientists believe that using and recognizing oneself in a mirror is a sign of complex cognitive processing and an indication of a level of awareness. Elephants, dolphins, primates, parrots, and even magpies recognize that it is themselves that they are seeing in the mirror's reflection. Pigs, too, are able to comprehend their reflections in a mirror. They will stare at their reflections, look from different angles, and be fascinated by the image of themselves. When researches hid food in such a way that the pigs could only see it through the reflection, seven out of eight pigs were able to find the food using the mirror to navigate their way to a meal.[25] Professor Donald Broom of Oxford University has stated that pigs "have the cognitive ability to be quite sophisticated. Even more so than dogs and certainly three-year-olds" (human children). Additionally, Dr. Mike Mendl of Bristol University said that "pigs can develop quite sophisticated social competitive behavior, similar to that seen in some primate species." The wide array of farmed animal emotion and intelligence is so often underestimated.[i]

Recently, a video circulated of a mother duck attempting to guide her five tiny ducklings across a hectic freeway. The harrowing, nail-biting scene was shown again and again on news stations and morning shows. Cars whizzed by at high speeds just inches from the feathered family, as they stuck together and cautiously waddled their way across the street. After an extremely distressing few seconds, they made it safely to the other side, as the viewers sighed with relief at the happy ending.

It is puzzling that while people are extremely concerned for the well-being of this family of ducks caught in a dangerous situation that day, most would have no reservations about going out and ordering a dead duck to eat at a Chinese restaurant that evening.

---

i Intelligence should not be a factor when we are considering whether animals are worthy of our compassion. It is far more relevant to ask whether they have the same ability to suffer, and the answer to this is an overwhelming affirmative. However, compassion or empathy tends to be a function of how much we relate to the recipient of our compassion—the more another being resembles our own species, the easier it is for people to feel compassion for him or her. We are only using intelligence—and not overall intelligence but specific factors of cognition—as one of the many ways that animals resemble humans to help elicit a sense of compassion. People who eat meat will often respond that it is okay to eat animals because "they are stupid"; however, this is simply not the case. Animals are, in fact, intelligent beings—even though ability to suffer, rather than intelligence, should be the main factor under consideration.

Why is it that they root for this mother duck to survive but have no concern for the bird who is to be their dinner? The duck on the plate likely had a more distressing life and certainly experienced a horrific death—just what the person watching the video was so concerned about. There is a cultural disconnect, a denial that the duck on the plate was ever a real duck, capable of fear and sorrow, able to love her ducklings and guide her family to safety, deserving of sympathy and concern. People will separate the meat on the plate from a living animal. Perhaps these mental acrobatics are a protection mechanism disconnecting them from the fact that they actually are concerned for the animal they eat; they choose to block it out, blindly eating *meat* and not an *animal*.

Yet, this sweet story is also hopeful in that we, as a society, are evolving a strong affinity for animals and don't want to see them suffer. If this video had been shown to evoke malicious expectation that the ducks would be hit and the viewer would be amused at the family's misfortune, we would not feel so optimistic—but that is not the case. The video was shown to evoke sympathy for the birds and to inspire relief and delight when they made it safely across the street. People were hoping the ducks would survive. Our endearing empathy for animals has grown in society, and our concern for their well-being is admirable. This is a promising sign in a violent world.

Another hopeful trend lies in the myriad stories of escaped animals. It seems to happen every few months or so that a cow will take matters into her own hooves and somehow escape her captors, usually while being transported, and send ranchers, law enforcement, animal control officers, and other would-be rescuers on a lively chase for hours or even days. As the media catches wind of a farm animal running amok and stopping traffic, they bring the story to the people, and sympathy starts to build for the errant cow. Folks hope that the animal will not be hurt in the process of her recapture, and he or she is frequently given a name. This animal desperado is no longer one of a thousand headed for the slaughterhouse, she is suddenly an individual caught in a distressing situation for everyone to see. We know her story, we know her plight, so we develop concern for her welfare. These animals usually end up at a sanctuary, spared from the horrible fate that originally awaited them.

A transport truck on the way to a Milwaukee slaughterhouse lost control and overturned with twenty-six cows in the cargo hold. In the commotion that followed, one cow was hit by another truck and others were shot or found dead near the crash site. But one lucky cow walked away and was on the run for a month before her recapture. She was called Bella, and her story of continuously eluding capture fascinated folks around the Northeast, where she was hiding out. She was finally corralled in a pasture and taken to SASHA Farm Animal Sanctuary outside Ann Arbor, Michigan, where they learned that they had rescued not one but two cows. Bella had been pregnant on her way to slaughter.

What is interesting about the stories of these escapees is that the plight of an individual farm animal is suddenly in the spotlight. With the media's continuous updates and people bearing witness and offering testimony, we are sympathetic to her dilemma and want the best outcome for her; we want her to be safely secured and to live out her life in peace. If farm animals' personal stories could be told, the stories of their suffering and sadness, their deprivation and fear, people would pay attention; they would care. This is why the animal agriculture industry operates in the dark, behind closed, locked doors. They know that if the public becomes aware of the misery farmed animals endure, consumers will start to ask questions, and seek alternatives—and that is exactly what is happening with animal consumption today. Concerned people are hearing about the horrors of factory farming and seeing images of sick and dying chickens piled on top of one another, of bloody piglets suffering on cold concrete floors, and heartless workers thrusting pitchforks into dairy cows' faces. They are becoming more aware of animal agriculture's impact on our planet and the heavy carbon hoofprint of raising billions of animals for food. In response, some caring consumers are seeking products advertised as "humane", "organic", and "sustainable"—and digging deeper in their wallets to pay for them.

We are making progress in our recognition of farmed animals' suffering and of their worth, but is alternative animal production the answer? Is it worth the extra money? Are the new methods of raising animals good for the planet? Is there really happy meat?

Part 1
The Ultimate Betrayal of Animals

Chapter 1
The Ethics of Betrayal

There comes a time when silence becomes betrayal.

—Martin Luther King Jr.

At the grocery store, products stretch from floor to ceiling with colorful packaging and enticing images. You can base your dizzying variety of food-purchasing choices on price, taste, quality, brand, and an assortment of other factors. Recently though, a new kind of shopper can be spotted roaming the grocery aisles and farmers' markets. These buyers take into account factors other than their personal needs and desires when making their food-buying decisions. These conscientious consumers think about the world around them and how their actions affect others. They have discovered that each product has a story, a narrative with potential impacts mixed in with the ingredients, and problems blended in the processing that touch lives beyond themselves and their families. These ethical shoppers examine each purchase, as each item has a power that can potentially cause suffering, destroy the environment, or harm life. They read labels. They pay attention. They care.

For many, shopping is a monotonous chore requiring little thought beyond lists, coupons, and prices. It is extremely admirable for someone to recognize the influence that purchasing power has on the larger world, on the animals that were part of the process, and the environmental effect of the product. This new way of consuming brings meaning to the mundane and is a significant way to shop. People aware of the potential impact of their consumer dollars recognize that money spent can either be funding suffering and destruction or casting a vote for something new—a more compassionate world of wholesome choices and a healthy environment.

These caring consumers deserve to know the whole truth about the new alternative animal products emerging on the market. Seeking humane and ecologically friendly choices are noble pursuits, and those who are willing to dig deeper in their wallets have the right to know the reality behind the labels. This book can help people to analyze the most ethical choices so that their time, effort, and desire to help alleviate suffering in the world will not be wasted. But before we analyze the details of alternative animal production and labeling, as will be explained in comprehensive detail in chapters 2 and 3, let's first examine the larger question: Can there really be happy meat, milk, or eggs?

Considering the proven capacity for animals to feel pain and experience emotional complexity, as discussed in the introduction, we may expect that when we become caretakers of domesticated animals, whether they are dogs, goats, or chickens we are leading these animals to believe that they can trust us. As with any relationship involving trust, there is an unspoken promise. These animals, as highly emotional beings, come to expect us to care for them, to make them as comfortable as we can, and to nurture them throughout their life stages. When we consistently feed them, give them water, and administer proper medical attention, they come to expect this humane treatment and develop a capacity for trust that can be truly astounding. This trust can lead to a sense of intense loyalty that is so strong it can be described as love.

But when the human guardian has an ulterior motive of self-interest and is all the while plotting to ultimately kill the animal companion for her flesh, this sacred bond of trust is completely violated by the human's treacherous motive. A violation of trust of this magnitude, when one individual depends on the other for her very life and every aspect of well-being, can only rightly be termed betrayal—the greater the degree of dependence, the greater the degree of trust, and the greater the bond of trust, the greater the magnitude of betrayal. Because these animals are so dependent on us, so trusting of us, and the violation of this incredible bond is an act so egregious, we have chosen to call it "the ultimate betrayal."

In the same way, abuse of children, the developmentally disabled, and the elderly is particularly egregious. These classes of individuals are dependent upon those who are responsible for their care, as their very survival depends on others. These groups of dependents would suffer gravely without the guardianship of individuals with greater capacities, abilities, and resources. And because the consequences of lack of care would be more severe, a violation of this trust constitutes a larger betrayal. Therefore, the degree of betrayal is a function of the degree of trust and dependence.

This brings us to the question of responsibility. A commitment to personal responsibility, above and beyond what is required by the law, is essential to the functioning of a peaceful and healthy society. Responsibility is proportional to need and resource; the greater the need of the object of responsibility, like a child or animal, and the greater the resource capacity of those capable of care, like a parent or guardian the heavier the burden of responsibility. Based on this formula it is when children are in infancy that they are most needy and thus when the parents' responsibility is greatest. It is when the elderly are frail and ill and the younger generation is experiencing the height of their independence and autonomy that their responsibility for care giving is at its upmost. It is when malnutrition is rampant and another class of society has a comfortable circumstance that responsibility to share is greatest.

In modern times animals have virtually no ability to control their environment, while humanity has been experiencing unrivaled hegemony over all other creatures as well as the very conditions of life on the planet. *Now* is the time for us to exercise our responsibility toward the less fortunate creatures that we share our planet with. If we, as humans, ever awaken to the ethical obligations that are an inherent function of the enjoyment of privilege, instead of selfishly asserting our traditions and desires at the expense of the welfare of other beings, then we will have achieved a society that will enjoy unprecedented harmony and peace with nature and with each other.

The word *humane* is commonly defined as being characterized by tenderness, compassion, and sympathy for people and animals, especially for the suffering or distressed.[1] This definition is completely antithetical to the act of treating animals as commodities instead of as sensitive and emotionally complex individuals. It is impossible to reconcile the principles of humane treatment with the inherently inhumane act of sending animals to slaughter, irrespective of how "good" a life they may have had. If one were to treat a person well and then murder him, the preceding "humane" treatment would do nothing to exonerate the killer of the crime, either morally or legally. At best the perpetrator might receive a sentence that is slightly less than that for a criminal who was guilty of murder *and* torture. But he would still receive a severe punishment for the killing. Imagine a defense attorney in a murder case making the argument that because the defendant treated his wife well before he killed her he should be acquitted of the horrendous crime. What would the jury say? What would *you* say? The perpetrator would still be guilty of murder, irrespective of how the victim was treated beforehand. Of course, it would be worse to be tortured and then killed, but nonetheless, there can be no benevolent killing, whether the victim is human or otherwise.[i] And killing is the more severe criminal act. Taking a sentient being's life for one's own interests can never be considered humane.

To look at it from another perspective, imagine if you were dependent on someone for your very survival. He is there in the early morning, providing your breakfast. He is there in the afternoon, tending to your living space. He comes back in the evening with more food. You are completely reliant on this person for your sustenance, your shelter, your very life. Like a child, you are dependent on his power to care for you. Now imagine that one day he comes to kill you and all your family and friends, or he ships you off to a death camp where you and your companions will be cruelly and thoughtlessly killed. Can you imagine the confusion, the sadness, the fear, the sense of *betrayal*? Would you thank this person for his past kind treatment, or would you curse him for his callous betrayal? The gravity of the betrayal would be so severe that you would not even feel a modicum of gratitude toward this person. You would realize he had simply been pretending to help you, while in fact he was only doing it for his own selfish motives. The magnitude of betrayal in the slaughter of animals is so great that it precludes any consideration of previous assistance

i Excepting, of course, the humane euthanasia of a severely injured or ill individual who has no hope of recovery.

provided to the animal. And because this assistance was not for the actual motive of helping the animal—rather, it was a means in the pursuit of self-serving intentions—these previous actions cannot be considered humane at all. More accurately, they were in the self-interest of the perpetrator, simply as a way to achieve selfish ends, that is, to have a "high-quality" meat product and make a profit.

Farm Sanctuary is a rescue and rehabilitation center, founded in 1993, where farmed animals who are injured, ill, or abused are nursed back to health by a caring and compassionate staff of employees and volunteers. The animals are allowed to live out their lives in peace on serene farms. Farm Sanctuary has three locations, with hundreds of animals in their guardianship and thousands more that come through for care and are adopted out. While you would assume that all the animals at the sanctuary come from the worst-of-the-worst abuse in large-scale, industrial factory farming, we found out that this is not the case at all.

Lil' Bud (Photo credit: Karen Gaines for Farm Sanctuary)

Lil' Bud

On our visit to Farm Sanctuary we met some gigantic, lethargic, and smiling pigs, who were not at all opposed to lifting a leg for a belly rub. We were told by Sophia Rivers, the education coordinator at the Orland, California sanctuary, that some of the pigs were rescued from a small family farm in New York one winter when Farm Sanctuary was tipped off that there was possible animal cruelty. The investigators found pigs huddled together, shivering, in the freezing sleet. Sophia said, "Some of the piglets were so cold that althoughthey were still alive, they were frozen to the ground."

The compassionate team was able to gently thaw them, rehabilitate them, and adopt some of them out. One of the survivors who has made his home at the sanctuary, Lil' Bud (not so little anymore!) was a soft-pink color with gentle, sleepy eyes. He rolled on his side, indolent in the summer heat, and let us scratch his globular belly.

Our tour guide pointed out how much the pigs adored the straw bedding and how they fluffed it with their snouts and made soft beds for afternoon siestas. She informed us that on factory farms the pigs are never given any bedding and have to lie on cold, hard, and often damp concrete or metal slatted floors. When asked if alternative farming operations offered bedding to pigs, she said that it varied from farm to farm. But Sophia's final thought was a poignant one: "Maybe the incentive for those farms that do give them bedding is to appeal to the buyer who is desperately searching for a compassionate choice." In other words, she was suggesting that if they do it at all, they do it for the consumer, and not for the animal himself.

This is the pattern among many so-called humane operations—they are not humane for the animals' sake; it is a marketing strategy to appease the conscience of consumers and to lure them into a false sense of confidence that no animals suffered for the product. If the producers were genuinely concerned about animals, they would not be in the business of killing animals. Ultimately, much of their "caring" is about appealing to a niche market where they can charge higher prices—they care about their bottom line.

Humane Slaughter?

It is curious that people will show great concern for how farmed animals are treated when alive and yet do not seem to be troubled by their slaughter. This fact seems to demonstrate a general inability to appraise the various gradations of moral transgressions, with killing being at the furthest end of the spectrum of immorality. Especially with respect to animal slaughter, there is a general tendency to ignore gradations of violent and harmful actions.

Our criminal justice system is based on the idea that punishment must be proportional to the crime, and we, as a society, have institutionalized varying gradations of punishment proportional to how serious we consider a crime to be. There is a general consensus that taking another's life is amongst the most serious type of crime.

In the United States, the death penalty is practiced in thirty-three of the fifty states and almost exclusively when the most horrible crime has been committed: murder.[2] Even then, extraneous circumstances must have also occurred—pre-meditation, kidnapping, rape, etc.—to warrant the death penalty. The extent to which our society values the human animals' life is highly admirable. Why is a nonhuman animal not afforded the same consideration? While we are certainly not advocating a position where people who kill animals receive the death penalty or are treated as murderers, there are compelling parallels between killing animals and killing humans. An animal has the same will to live as a human does. And, as stated in the introduction, they have much of the same consciousness, awareness, and emotional capacity. Are they really so different?

In our tendency to deny farmed animals a place in our circle of compassion, we fail to properly assess the gravity of the act of killing and tend to exclusively consider the conditions in which an animal lives. There is a sense that it is okay to slaughter an animal as long as she has been treated well, the "one-bad-day" scenario. In this sentiment, we fall short of extending the same recognition to animals that is the cornerstone of our criminal justice system: that taking life is the highest transgression, much worse than any crime that allows for the survival of the victim. For example, would you rather have six months in a five-star hotel and then be executed or have a lifetime in jail? Most everyone would take the lifetime in prison, even if the conditions were harsh. Because animals share similar behaviors to humans regarding their will to live, it is safe to assume that they would share the preference for living as well. Life is an animal's most cherished possession and animals, like humans, will fight to survive. It is absurd to speak of humane treatment of animals when it comes to their handling, management, food, and shelter if you deny them the most basic right—to live out their lives—and condone or are complicit in their slaughter. Clearly, the killing of the animal is the most severe transgression, greater than any mistreatment that allows the victim to live. And because of that, our greatest concern should not necessarily be the treatment of the animal, though this is obviously very important; rather, the greatest consideration should be that the animal be allowed to live.

To propose another question: Would you rather be murdered or assaulted with a baseball bat? Even though being hit with a baseball bat would be very painful or potentially debilitating, most rational people, if faced with this horrible choice, would prefer to be victimized in a way that allowed them to live. Even if there is no assurance of full recovery (excepting cases where there is ongoing and irreversible suffering) it is preferable to live, because most people value life above all other considerations of well-being. This is a value that animals share, and it should be extended to them. To illustrate the point differently: Would you hit a pig with a baseball bat? Of course not, and it would be unacceptable for a rancher to do so, also. So why is it acceptable to inflict the greater violation—killing the pig? As a society we tend to consider the lesser infraction of animal cruelty to be a much greater moral wrong than the much greater transgression of killing, and somehow we find it acceptable to condone the killing of animals that are marketed as humanely raised. Labeling killing "humane" is as contradictory as calling the lifeless remains "happy."

The consideration that killing is the worst of transgressions is not limited to humans in our society. Our comprehensive anti-cruelty laws for companion animals also follow this logical progression. Captain Cindy Machado, Director of Animal Services for over twenty-nine years at the Marin Humane Society in Novato, California, has explained that the severity of animal cruelty has a bearing on the level of the charges against the person responsible for the crime. Captain Machado said, "In the maximum punishments we've seen, the animal has to have been brutally injured or killed. That makes a difference whether or not cases are charged at the felony level or just a charge of a misdemeanor." She added, "If an animal is killed as a result of abuse or neglect, the punishment is likely to be more severe." It is considered cruelty, so extreme that you could acquire a felony charge and jail time, if you kill a dog[ii]—but kill hundreds of cows a day, and you get a paycheck.

We have made farmed animals exempt from our basic moral understandings of the degree and severity of offenses and have somehow compensated for this nagging, unconscious compunction

---

ii Unless the dog is legally euthanized in a shelter. However, the point is the same. If it is wrong to kill an individual animal, then it should be worse to kill large numbers of animals, irrespective of their species.

with the compromise that farm animals must at least be treated well while alive. This is a good first step in bringing to our conscious awareness the admission of their suffering, but the logical extension of this thinking is that we should not kill them at all, as killing is the worst of all the acts we can commit against one another.

There is a strong disparity between the enjoyment that we receive from consuming animal flesh and the sacrifice that an animal has given to provide this pleasure. We receive relatively little, and the animal is forced to give everything. This is a complete inequality for the animal who has been killed for the momentary indulgence. Such a fleeting enjoyment cannot match the value of the permanent state that is death, and therefore the animal has given much more than the consumer has received. This is injustice. Robert Grillo eloquently wrote in his blog Free From Harm, "and even when the human interest is trivial and the animal interest is a matter of life and death—as in the case of satisfying our palate pleasure—we still place our interest over theirs. And we do this automatically because that's how it's always been done—not because we've really given any serious moral consideration to the issue—but simply because we can."[3]

The idea that you can humanely kill an animal is completely absurd. The very act of killing is the greatest source of inhumanity and the worst act of violence. Based on the formulation of betrayal articulated above, the more humanely an animal is treated, the greater is the bond of trust, and the greater the bond of trust, the more severe the crime of betrayal. By this standard, killing "humanely" treated animals could be a much greater act of betrayal.

This does not imply that it is more ethical to abuse and then kill an animal, because in this scenario there is no element of betrayal.

Rather, this is only to posit that regardless of how the animal is treated there is a moral transgression. If the animal is treated well before slaughter, then betrayal is the infraction preceding the act of killing. If the animal is treated badly, then abuse is the preceding crime. Either way, if animals are raised for the purpose of ending their life to serve the interests of the human captor, regardless of how the animal is treated, whether abused or betrayed, it is wrong.

While violence is undoubtedly a severe criminal act, some might argue that betrayal is even worse. In Dante Alighieri's fourteenth-century epic poem *Divine Comedy*, the first part, entitled *Inferno*, famously reserves the deepest of the nine circles of hell for the betrayer, while violence is only considered the seventh, followed by fraud, which is the eighth. Because these concentric circles represent a gradual increase in wickedness, Dante is issuing a clear statement: to covertly deceive with malicious intention is even worse than an overt act of violence. Perhaps this distinction is subjective, but it is important to note that violence, betrayal, and fraud are all committed in the act of killing an animal, especially one with whom we've developed a bond of trust (betrayal) and one that will be labeled humane (fraud). Yet we find on "alternative" farms that most animals are not at all humanely treated, despite misleading labeling to the contrary. We will delve deeper into this deception in chapters 2 and 3.

There can be no such thing as happy meat. Meat is dead. It has no emotion. However, it came from a living, breathing, sentient being who had the capacity for happiness; one assumes that this is what the folks who use this term mean—that the living animal, before he became a piece of meat, was happy. But this just perpetuates the fatal flaw in the entire concept of eating animals and animal products. One day soon, no matter how happy the animal is, she will be dead. And no sentient being is happy to be killed. On the contrary, any animal will fight to live. Death is an unhappy option—an unwelcome prospect. Animals desire to continue living. The concept of happy meat is erroneous, and as will be revealed in the following chapters, "happy" farmed animal operations are anything but.

Unless you were with an animal through her entire life and accompanied her to the slaughterhouse you do not know what kind of life or death she had. It is impossible to really know. Manufacturers will tell stories that pacify, labels show pictures that appease, and websites offer fabrications that soothe the conscience. If you cannot be sure, don't take the risk, because the animal behind the delightful label was not happy and may have suffered considerably. The industry will lie to sell products.

The idea of being an ethical meat eater or a compassionate carnist[iii],[4] has inherent contradictions. This is not to say that people who consume animal products are fundamentally without compassion or ethics. People can be extremely compassionate and ethical in some areas of life, such as when it comes to children, the poor, the environment, companion animals, etc., and then go home and eat a cheeseburger. The implications of this later action contradict the values expressed in the previous actions. I have seen friends weep over the loss of a dog or cat, but then shed no tears for the animal

---

iii *Why We Love Dogs, Eat Pigs and Wear Cows,* Melanie Joy, Conari Press, 2010, pp. 29–30. Joy writes: "We eat animals without thinking about what we are doing and why, because the belief system that underlies this behavior is invisible. This invisible belief system is what I call carnism … Carnism is the belief system in which eating certain animals is considered ethical and appropriate. Carnists—people who eat meat are not the same as carnivores. Carnivores are animals that are dependent on meat to survive … Carnists eat meat not because they need to, but because they choose to, and choices always stem from beliefs."

they will eat that day who certainly suffered much more than their dog or cat. If they knew the pig, and the misery she endured, they would likely also be distressed by her life cut short merely for a meal. Most people have compassion for helpless beings and don't want to see them die, but their window of compassion is only open for certain species. Open the window wide and let farm animals into your sight of concern. Farmed animals have the same ability to suffer as any other animal and they are worthy of our sympathy, just like an injured bird that fell from a nest, just like a starving, stray dog. We would offer assistance to these animals if it was within our abiltiy to help them—why are pigs, cows, and chickens exempt from this compassion? How can we, in good conscience, kill when it is unnecessary?[iv] Causing another's death when there is no benefit to our health or to the planet, and indeed, when it is harmful to the environment and our bodies, simply is not consistent with the dictates of ethical living. We must widen our circle of compassion to embrace all nonhuman animals.

---

iv It is important to realize that we should not pretend that it is possible to entirely abstain from the process of killing. Irrespective of what we choose to eat, some animals are killed in the process. Even in the cultivation of plant foods, insects are killed, the environment and wildlife can be jeopardized, and human workers may be exploited. We must not pretend that we can somehow be so perfect that we do not participate in killing at all. However, there is a gradation, and people who are conscious of the effects of their actions can follow the axiom of least harm. It is easy to see how there is excessive and unnecessary killing involved in the production of animal foods. There is infinitely less carnage in plant production than in animal agriculture, so the clear ethical choice is to reduce or abstain from animal foods.

Elsa (photo credit: Animal Place)

Elsa

We visited another farm animal sanctuary called Animal Place, located on a beautiful six-hundred-acre spread in Grass Valley, California. There we met Elsa, a caramel-colored cow with a gentle look in her eye. She loves a good scratch on the head and down her back; she will offer an approving glance back for your kind touch. Our tour guide, Marji Beach, has been with Animal Place for over seven years. She explained that Elsa was from a Waldorf School, an alternative charter-type school that encourages hands-on learning. She was used to teach dairy production, with a few other cows, in a small operation on the school grounds. After Elsa had seen fifteen years of students' affection, the school purchased four draft horses and determined that Elsa took up too much space and that they didn't want to feed her anymore. Marji told us that, at the age of fifteen, after being adored by children, being loved, and named, and having that positive interaction with people, she was going to be sent to slaughter. Animal Place normally focuses on rescuing neglected and abused farmed animals and doesn't usually take in animals people are trying to "get rid of" because they're tired of caring for the animals. They focus mostly on farm rescues, but Marji explained, "We just couldn't say no to this cow who had known nothing but kindness from people and to know that she would be betrayed in such an awful way was just heart wrenching." The Animal Place staff recognized that to betray Elsa now by sending her to slaughter, after she had been loved and cared for for so many years, would be exceptionally tragic. She deserved to live the rest of her life out in peace, never to know the terrible truth of the heartbreaking fate of most of her kind. It somehow seemed preferable to keep her in blissful ignorance, reinforcing her mistaken impression that humanity is entirely compassionate, kind, and loving.

Human Superiority

A species cannot necessarily be ranked in terms of superiority or inferiority any more than one culture, gender, or race can be categorized as superior to another. We can, however, talk about superior capacities that various species possess, which may not necessarily lead to the conclusion that one species is superior, in much the same way that we can conclude that one culture may have more advanced technology without necessarily implying that it is a superior culture.

It should not be controversial to assert that humans have superior capacities to other animals in many ways. Humans certainly are unique in their ability to willfully dominate and control the destinies of virtually every other species on the planet. Humans are able to manipulate the natural world to create an environment befitting our needs, making it more comfortable and entertaining with each passing year. All of these factors contribute to our status of possessing superior capacities in the sense that we possess greater capacities of reason that allow for highly complex manipulations of our external environment. However, as a species, we tend to think that superior capacity equals superiority, much the way the advanced capabilities to create technology led European colonists to dominate and exterminate indigenous populations during the period of European imperialism.

However, such ability to manipulate the environment cannot always be viewed as leading to improvements. Human manipulation of the environment is, by definition, to be considered an artificial enhancement. This artificially created environment can only be considered superior insofar as it is able to suit the whims of the dominant human species. But artificial manipulations often do not allow for the biological stability and complexity of a climax community or for ecological harmony. Our artificial environments also separate us from the natural world, especially when our actions are at odds with the needs of animals, creating an increasing chasm between human and nonhuman beings. As most animals do not seem to be part of our everyday life, this rift makes it hard for us to care about other species and the natural world.

Along with our superior capacity as humans to manipulate the environment comes the superior facility to weigh decisions and explore multiple options when we make our choices. This accounts for our greater responsibility for the well-being of the Earth. Choice leads to ethics and ethics to responsibility. Our intellectual capacities[v] also carry with them the potential for humanity to act in a way that is inferior to any other being on the planet, such as when we act immorally and disregard the needs of others for our own selfish interests.

While other species may also exhibit behaviors such as selfishness, cruelty, etc., they do not possess the advanced rational capacities that humans do, and therefore their behavior cannot be considered unethical, at least not to the same extent. The greater the capacity for rational behavior, the weightier is the value judgment that can be placed on that behavior. Following this logic, when a child lies or steals, the action does not carry as much gravity as when an adult does. Therefore, humans, who possess perhaps the greatest rational capacity, have the potential to achieve the most ethical behavior but also to commit the most unethical atrocities. Because animals lack this superior faculty to weigh decisions, our greater intellectual capacity can be said to be superior only if we act ethically. The second that we act immorally, we have degraded our status and become inferior to other animals, largely because we have a choice to act otherwise. This capacity for conscience and ethical choice is our species' ultimate advantage. If humans are able to stop and ponder the decisions that we make, shouldn't we then be making the choices that will cause the least suffering? That will preserve and protect the planet? That will make our bodies healthy? Only if we make higher ethical choices can the faculty of intellectual reason be said to be superior; otherwise this very capacity could make us the most inferior species alive

---

v This is not to say that *all* of our intellectual capacities as humans are superior, rather that *some* of our intellectual capacities are superior, and perhaps other capacities of animals may very well exceed our own.

today—because we are the only species that has the capacity to act unethically to such an extreme extent.

A key element in our evolution has been the ability to pause and think about what we are doing, and consciously decide to make the best choice. However, for most of that time, humanity has restricted this ability to selfish choices: what *I* want, what will make *me* comfortable, what tastes good to *me*. This has brought us to a point where billions of animals suffer every day in animal agriculture, and the planet is on the brink of disaster, with climate change causing annual storms of the century. Given the state of disaster we humans have wrought upon the planet, it seems an argument can be made for the inferiority of the human intellectual capacity of reason. No animal species has ever screwed things up this badly.

We are at a defining moment when we can consciously shift from the self-serving choices that have been the central characteristic of the human legacy to ones that benefit not only humanity as a whole but other species and the entire planet, as well. Only then can we talk about human superiority in any meaningful way.

To be consistent with this voice of inner conscience, it is not enough to demand that food animals be treated fairly and humanely while they are alive; we must abstain entirely from participation in their killing in any form, including providing financial support to animal-killing industries. Discomfort with animal suffering leads to the inescapable conclusion that one should not participate in killing. And nonparticipation largely implies not providing financial support to these businesses. Simply demanding sufficient exposure to outdoors, fresh air, food, and shelter, and then being complicit in the termination of their lives, is morally inconsistent (although it is still imperative that we make these former demands). The dissonance between the voice of conscience and the contradiction of adhering to the status quo of participating in the killing of animals is not only immoral but ultimately has significant repercussions on our own psychological health. To be psychologically healthy, our values and principles must reflect a harmonious consistency. Therefore, we cannot simultaneously be repulsed by cruelty and participate in the atrocity of taking life, while still expecting to find any sense of psychological well-being.[5]

Carmen (photo credit: Animal Place)

Carmen

Continuing on our tour of Animal Place, we reached a pasture with a cluster of sheep grazing on a gently sloping, lovely hillside. Some of the sheep had exceptionally long tails, almost reaching the ground—an unusual sight, as most domesticated sheep have their tails cut off. Soon, the cutest little sheep ever came to greet us! But her locomotion was a pathetic and labored hop on only three legs. She was missing her front left leg.

Six-month-old Carmen came from a small farm that used sheep as weed eaters. Soon after she was born, she severely injured her leg, probably by tripping in a hole. The farmer felt that he couldn't afford to treat her, so she stumbled around on a broken leg for two weeks until a concerned neighbor was able to take the lamb to the safety of Animal Place. They took her to UC Davis Veterinary Hospital, but after a grueling week of two surgeries and isolation, it was evident that her leg was completely damaged beyond hope and had to be amputated. It's an unfortunate reality that many small farms don't have the money and resources to properly care for their animals, and as is often the case in animal farming, injuries are ignored and sicknesses go untreated.

In this case, the neglect cost one little lamb her leg, but because of the concern of a neighbor and the diligence of caring advocates, her life was saved. This story shows that even when the animal is not being directly consumed, facilities that use animals as part of an industrial enterprise can still be complicit in cruelty to animals through neglect, regardless of the status of that farm as being small, local, organic, etc. Therefore, it is best to avoid supporting any farms that include the exploitation of animals as a means to economic ends.

Visceral Veganism

Imagine sitting down to a plate of food. Wouldn't you think that you should be able to picture the entire process of how that food arrived at your plate *while you eat it?* If you are eating a plate of, let's say, spaghetti with tomato sauce, there is no problem in picturing the tomato, spinach, and wheat seeds being planted: the plants growing; the crops being harvested; the processing, packaging, and cooking would all be informative to watch.[vi]

Now imagine if there were meatballs in the spaghetti. Could you watch the entire process of how they got there while eating that plate of food? Could you watch the artificial insemination, where a farmer inserts his entire arm in the cow's rectum while feeling around for the insemination tool that is being inserted in the vagina with the other arm? Could you watch the animal being born and then, just a short time later, being shot in the head with a bolt gun? Could you eat while she is hoisted up by one leg and her throat slit? Could you put food in your mouth while her blood drains on the floor? Could you witness as the feet and head are cut off, her body sliced open, and the innards and entrails tumble out of her? Could you enjoy your meal as the organs are wrenched out and the muscle is pulled from the bone? Most people would have a hard time keeping a meal down while watching the slaughtering process. Does it make any sense that we should then eat this animal? If we can't stomach the process and eat at the same time, then perhaps we should not be partaking in it after the gore is cleaned up and hidden from view.

---

vi This visualization is focused primarily on the processing of plants and does not take into account any human rights violations of workers, pesticide use, etc. which could taint the positive or neutral experience of watching the process of growing and harvesting plants.

Another perplexing ritual is the standard centerpiece at many a Thanksgiving table, the whole turkey. Featherless and headless, the bird lies on his back, often with his body full of stuffing. But where is that stuffing stuffed? The anus and colon have been removed, but you are still stuffing the bird in his anal cavity. Clearly there is a disgusting element here, one that is in plain sight, but people choose not to think about it. However, once this repugnant revelation is brought to one's attention, it's hard to look at the Thanksgiving meal in quite the same way.

There are some parts of the animal that most people in the United States find offensive to eat, such as the tongue, feet, liver, and chitlins (the intestines). They are horribly disgusted by the idea of eating these parts of the animal, yet for some reason, the muscle tissue is the acceptable section of the body to eat. But is there really so much difference from one body part to another? Most meat-eating animals chomp the raw, bloody body whole—eyes, brains, organs, genitals and all. We seem to be so repulsed by eating a dead animal that we cut him up carefully, drain his blood, separate out anything we find offensive, choose only certain parts of the body as suitable to eat, and cook those parts thoroughly, wasting the rest. Then there is the disturbing fact that there is fecal matter on almost every piece of meat[6]— including 92 percent of chicken carcasses[7]—and pus present in nearly all dairy products.[8] This health hazard is explored further in chapter 10.

We apologize for the crude nature of this argument, but are you appetized by the by-products of an animal's reproductive process? Have you ever considered eating the ovulation or mammary secretions of another animal? Does that sound delicious? Of course not, but that is exactly what eggs and dairy are. The consumption of reproductive fluids of animals (i.e., eggs and dairy) is only palatable if we are desensitized by a thorough process of acculturation. So it is likely that a culture whose survival depends on ingesting rat milk or the ovulation cycle excretions (eggs) of platypuses would have no problem doing so. It may sound strange to us, but to them it would be quite normal. Likewise, if we abstain from ingesting eggs and dairy for an extended time, then we will likely realize how strange this custom really is. If we were to unravel our cultural conditioning and see eggs and dairy for what they are, then we would find that we are as viscerally disgusted by these products as we are by any other biological by-product of an animal's reproductive process. Before you eat it, just think for a moment about where that egg and dairy came from.

It is important to note that this is not the case for plant matter. There is no part of a plant that we are viscerally disgusted by in the same way. Sure, we may have become sick from eating a rotten tomato and then not like tomatoes, but that is a process of learned association, not something that is as inherent as, say, the prospect of drinking dog milk. Why is cow milk so different?

The argument for visceral veganism is not necessarily based on intellectual reasoning or ethical consideration. This is an argument that is based on experience and "gut instinct." Our modern culture has a bias in favor of intellect-based information while ignoring urges, impulses, and signals that may be delivered to our conscious intellectual center of decision-making. Of course, the rise of hyper-intellectualism has had the indispensable benefit of leading society away from superstition and irrational beliefs that are generally harmful and ignorant. We certainly encourage choosing scientific fact over fabrication. But we would argue that just because a certain feeling doesn't seem rational that does not necessarily make it irrational.

For example, there are many wild plants that just simply taste bad. Often they are astringent because, despite being edible in smaller quantities, they contain various toxic compounds that could make us sick if eaten in large quantities. We could rationally argue that they are more natural than our standard agricultural variety of vegetable and therefore must be better for us. But it would be unwise to conclude that our taste buds were behaving irrationally (contrary to our rational assumptions) and therefore ignore the signals. Likewise, there are times when we react spontaneously, bypassing the slow and cumbersome mechanisms of the rational intellect, and are all the better because of it, as when you react in traffic to avoid an accident. We may have irrational-seeming associations that lead us to dislike foods, but these may actually be protective mechanisms to avoid foods that we are allergic to or that are dangerous, such as raw meat. Most people certainly are disgusted by the act of slaughtering and processing of dead animals. Perhaps it's a little too close to home; after all, we are all animals.

Because this signal is so strong and ubiquitous amongst a majority of people, and the overwhelming evidence exists that animal foods increase the risk of chronic degenerative disease, it would be wise to listen to our visceral response to witnessing the violent act of killing and to refrain from partaking of food that disgusts us when we witness its production. We should listen to our gut feelings. Obviously, this is not to say that the converse is true, that because something looks appealing and delicious that it must be good for the body. Of course this not the case, as any science-based analysis of junk food and sugary desserts would suggest.

The Power of Language

There is a simple, yet profound, action one can take to help create a more ethical world. Simply use the term *animal guardian* instead of the term *animal owner*. The paradigm shift resulting from a conscious change in language can have far-reaching, positive effects on our relationship to animals, and it will instill a greater sense of respect, responsibility, and compassion toward farmed animals in particular.

Our word choices define not only who we are and what we believe in but also who we want to be. The words we choose convey our underlying values and how we hope to progress as a society. Gandhi said, "The greatness of a nation and its moral progress can be judged by the way its animals are treated." In our current language, we "own" other sentient beings. This is conceptually related to slavery. White men no longer *own* other men of color; men no longer *own* their wives or their children. Animals are the next logical extension of this recognition that sentient beings deserve to be free of oppression.

You own a car or a lamp or a nightstand. But animals in our care, like children, deserve our safeguarding. We are their protectors— their guardians. "Owners" are free to use their property however they choose and dispose of *it* whenever they want. Guardians recognize animals as individuals, not objects. Marc Bekoff said in *Minding Animals,* "Animals are not property or 'things' but rather living organisms, subjects of a life, who are worthy of our compassion, respect, friendship, and support." If *owner* is not the right word to use when referring to animal companions, why would it be appropriate when applied to animals raised for food?

This moral shift in thinking helps us view animals as more than mere property, objects, or things to be bought and sold. Changing one's language to represent oneself as a guardian, rather than as an owner or master, demonstrates a respectful, compassionate viewpoint and shows others that animals are not ours to abuse, neglect, or slaughter, but to cherish and protect.

It is also important to use *he* and *she* whenever we are referring to an animal—not *it*. Ships and hurricanes are universally referred to as *she*, yet we generally call a dog or a cow or a monkey *it*. Perhaps subconsciously attaching the word *it* to animals makes it easier to deny their suffering and their feelings, making it easier to exploit them. It is less problematic to eat, wear, and experiment upon an *it* rather than a *he* or *she*. *Its* are things, and things can be owned. The days of owning sentient beings should be over.

If someone is called a guardian of egg-laying hens, the job is defined. That person must guard them, care for their needs, and protect them from dangers—certainly not kill them as their egg production declines. The importance of language cannot be overstated. It affects how we think and how we act. The gentle beings who ask so little deserve the reverence, protection, and care the term guardian represents.

Perhaps one could accuse animal advocates of over-humanizing—or anthropomorphizing—animals. However, given that animals have similar capacity to ours to feel pain and emotion, terms such as *humanity* and *altruism*, which are traditionally reserved to human behavior, should be expanded to include the behavior of animals as well. Why can't animals behave altruistically or with humanity? These terms represent a virtue of demonstrating love and kindness even to the point of self-sacrifice. Because these virtues of humanity and altruism can be observed amongst most animals in their treatment of each other and toward different species, it would be appropriate for us to extend our definition of these words to include the behavior of nonhumans as both subjects and objects of these qualities. Indeed, it is not unreasonable to speak of the humanity of animals or of animals behaving altruistically. Likewise, it is not unreasonable to speak of having a sense of humanity or altruism toward nonhuman species.

Even the term *meat* is a euphemistic way of describing the flesh of an animal. The word meat originally simply meant food, excluding drink.[9] Current usage of the term describes some plant foods, as in nut meats. Its etymological usage did not exclusively refer to food from animal sources. It is interesting to wonder why in modernity animal foods are not described as *flesh*, *corpse*, or *carcass*. Animal advocates are accused of using dysphemistic terms when they employ such terminology. Perhaps this is so, but these later descriptions come closer to capturing the entire process of the object in question, instead of just its final stage, on a plate. Therefore, such truthful terms offer a more complete and accurate description of what an animal product is. It is fair to say that most people would be less enticed by these appellatives. When it is called meat it has the association with food, and therefore its edible connotation subordinates the predominate definition that the term flesh offers, suggesting the tissue of a dead animal. But which designation is more accurate? The term meat has something to hide, while the term flesh is a more honest designation.

One could go on to call milk lactic fluid or bodily secretion and eggs a chicken's ovulatory discharge, but the point is the same. Convention has attached labels to these substances that emphasize their edible qualities at the expense of a more impartial description of what they really are, essentially using language to mask the revulsion behind the food on our plates. A closer examination of how our labels desensitize us to the terrible truth behind the entire animal production process would be beneficial to our evolution as a species. Call it what it is—flesh, corpse, muscle tissue, ovum, mammary secretion, etc.—and see how much you still want to eat it. A just and compassionate world can begin with a more accurate use of language.

Chapter 2
Is Alternative Animal Production Humane?

Whenever people say "We mustn't be sentimental,"
you can take it they are about to do something cruel.
And if they add "We must be realistic," they mean
they are going to make money out of it.

—Brigid Brophy

When we drive by a cow casually munching grass in a field, we might reflect on the peaceful scene and consider that she doesn't have it so bad. But what we are seeing is a brief snapshot in her life. What happened before that moment, what certainly will happen after, and what is hidden from the consumer is the greater concern if we are truly interested in a holistic picture of the welfare of farmed animals. The growing trend in animal agriculture for products to appear humane and environmentally sustainable is gaining momentum. Producers of animal meat, dairy, and eggs are describing new products with a range of pacifying labels like Free Range, Organic, Natural, and other classifications with images of lush, grassy hills and clean, open barns to entice customers to buy their products. The local burger joint offers grass-fed beef burgers. There are cage-free eggs listed on the ingredients in a muffin at the coffee shop. Go to any natural food store and you will see that humane and sustainable choices abound, but what do they really mean? What is the whole story surrounding this new way of farming animals? Does it, in fact, solve the ethical and environmental problems of raising animals for food?

This rising awareness is moving us toward a more compassionate culture, and it is an encouraging sign that we, as a society, are now acknowledging that animals do suffer to produce meat, milk, and eggs. However, the unfortunate reality is that animals on an alternative operation suffer many of the same cruel practices as their factory-farmed cousins, and slaughter is still the end result. It is important to note that these alternative farming operations only account for a small fraction of the animal products available on the market today, and if someone is eating animal products daily, it is unlikely that they are getting them entirely from alternative sources.

The difference between commercial operations and alternative operations can range from very slight to more significant, but there are certain inherent cruelties in any animal agriculture operation that cannot be avoided. There are numerous horrible and heartless agricultural practices that are universal and essential to making a profit. Alternative operations cannot circumvent such practices, and the consumer is left uninformed, unaware, and assuaged by the reassuring label.

Captain Cindy Machado, a twenty-nine-year veteran of the Marin Humane Society, explains that there is a substantial difference between what species an animal is and what the law considers cruelty to that animal. She explains, "When you look at what someone can do to a dog and what someone can do to a cow on a farm, they are on opposite extremes. There are acts of cruelty that go on every day on all farms, 'happy' farms and factory farms alike, acts of husbandry that are acts of cruelty that, if you did to a dog, you would get thrown in jail." There is an agricultural exemption, sometimes referred to as "reasonable care standard" where industry deems certain practices necessary and commonplace and therefore they are not considered cruel, even though they certainly are. Captain Machado continues, "Some of the common, every day practices on any farm—whether it's branding, or ripping toes off, or ear tagging, or ear notching, or debeaking, all without anesthetics—all those activities that are day-to-day, common things, have been ignored, and those animals are experiencing the same level of pain and suffering that a dog or cat would, and it's not viewed as cruelty." Which species an animal is dictates how well he or she is protected by law or even whether he or she is protected at all. Machado concludes with this disconcerting thought, "And in the case of most of the farm animal issues that we have seen over the years, they are far from being protected."

"Alternative" Dairy Production

To produce a profitable dairy product, the well-being of the animal will have to be compromised in some fundamental ways, no matter how humane an operation claims to be. Mammals do not produce milk unless they are pregnant or have recently been pregnant. "Alternative" dairies still have to keep the cows or goats pregnant every year to produce the maximum amount of milk, far more than is natural for their bodies. This is most always accomplished through artificial insemination, performed by invasively inserting a long metal device called an inseminating gun into the cow's vagina. At the same time, the rancher inserts his other arm in her rectum, almost to his shoulder, to manipulate the vaginal wall with his hand for insemination.[1] This violation must be at the least uncomfortable, and is likely a painful and frightening experience for a young cow.

Being constantly pregnant year after year puts a strain on the cow's body, and her health will suffer from the intense exploit. In so-called humane dairies, calves are still taken from their mothers at birth.[2] This is perhaps the greatest grief any living being could suffer, evidenced by how the mother and calf will often mourn sorrowfully and forcefully protest the separation, especially if there has been any time allowed for them to bond. As a result, the calves are typically taken away immediately at birth to prevent bonding. A strong connection forms between a mother with her unborn offspring, and to have the baby taken away directly after birth creates a state of extreme psychological trauma. Why is it that dairy producers tear apart bovine families and have the calves grow up as orphans, without the love or comfort of a mother? It's because they cannot have the calf drinking the sellable product.

Bella the dairy cow, whom we met in the introduction, gave birth to her son, Mr. Rogers, soon after arriving at the SASHA Farm Animal Sanctuary. The two were inseparable. About six months after his birth, Mr. Rogers suffered a torn ligament in his leg. He was removed for veterinary care, and Bella, in obvious distress, forcefully bellowed for him all night. He, in turn, agonizingly called for his mother. The next day he was returned to her and they ran to each other, Bella nuzzling him in welcome, and again they became inseparable. This was the first time one of her offspring was ever returned to her. In the production of dairy products for human consumption, mothers and babies are always separated, an inherent cruelty in the dairy operation.

Usually, after calves are taken away from their dairy cow mothers, the baby females are chained outside, regardless of weather conditions, to calf hutches, which resemble white plastic doghouses. Isolated from the other calves and without the care of their mothers, they are kept like this, alone and frightened, chained and unloved. Once old enough, they experience their own violation, in the form of artificial insemination, so they can become pregnant and begin to lactate, the sole purpose of their lives at the hands of their human captors. Ironically, the milk that should be going to nourish a baby calf is instead sold as a human product, and consumers are so dazzled by idyllic pictures of rolling pastures and grazing cows that they never see the horrible mistreatment of the animal behind the mammary secretions that they consume.

Male babies born to a dairy-producing mother are nothing more than a waste product of the dairy industry. They obviously cannot produce milk, so keeping these adorable and gentle creatures around to consume their mother's milk, their natural food, is simply not cost effective. That would be "wasting" the milk the producers could otherwise sell. So, like their sisters, male calves will be ripped from their mothers at birth, never to know their comfort and security. They will never frolic in a field, the birthright of all baby ruminants. Even at the supposedly best commercial operations, like American Humane certified Clover Dairy, they still have to get rid of the baby males, sending them to auction just one week after birth, for veal, or to be raised for low-quality beef, most likely not on an alternative operation.[3] Auctions are loud, frightening places for any animal, especially a terrified newborn. A former auction worker confided, "They drag newborn calves that still have their umbilical cords, dragging them by the ears, by the tail, calves that are too weak to stand on their own, and they just drag them around and off the trucks." Words can only convey so much of the true horrors of the auction yard; please go to the resource page at the back of this book and learn where to find videos.

About one third of veal calves, the undesired male (and some female) babies of the dairy industry, are kept in tiny crates, where they can't turn around or lie down comfortably. They are tethered by the neck, can barely move, and have been put on a liquid diet that doesn't have adequate iron, so it keeps their muscles underdeveloped and their flesh white and tender. Others are in small group pens, longing for their mothers, and unable to run, play, or feel the sun or wind on their bodies. After just about twenty-two to twenty-four weeks of misery, these babies are slaughtered for veal.[4] Many people recognized the cruelty of killing baby cows and won't eat veal, yet they continue to ingest dairy, not knowing the intimate connection between the industries. One supports the other and there is extreme cruelty in both.

Through selective breeding, a modern dairy cow can produce about ten times as much milk as her ancestors did generations ago. Milk yield per cow increased by 95 percent from 1950 to 1975 and grew an additional 76 percent from 1975 to 2000.[5] Dairy cows are now producing much more milk than was ever intended by the natural design specifications of their bodies. They used to produce just over a gallon each, about eight and a half pounds, just enough to nourish a calf. Now they are nourishing American obesity at an astonishing sixty to one hundred pounds of milk a day.

A dairy animal is not offered a retirement plan. Humane or not, modern dairy production is terribly taxing on her body, and it is just not profitable to keep her around when she is not producing as much milk as the younger cows, the daughters that she will never nuzzle or care for. After about three lactating cycles, her milk output wanes, and she will be sent to slaughter and be sold for ground beef and other low-quality meat products. Many fast-food hamburgers are made from "spent" dairy cows. With a natural lifespan of about twenty years, they are killed in the human equivalent of their preteens. Even on the so-called humane farms, a few favorites may be "retired," but it is not profitable to feed them if they are not producing, and most will go to slaughter.[6] It is impossible for a farm to create a truly humane environment— wherein families are allowed to stay together, express their normal behaviors, and live out their natural life spans—*and* make a profit. A viable business model cannot avoid the inherent cruelties of dairy production. The only way to be truly humane is a widespread cultural shift away from consumption of animal products.

Colleen Patrick-Goudreau, author of several books on compassionate eating, had this to say about dairy production:

"Because a cow's life is only as valuable as the offspring and amount of milk she is able to produce, when she is no longer profitable (i.e., when the costs to feed, medicate, and shelter her exceed the revenue derived from her milk output), she is sent to slaughter. Whether she is used on a small farm, organic farm, family-owned farm, artisan farm, or whatever-it's-called-farm, she is sent to slaughter. Whether the milk is labeled organic, whole, pasteurized, unpasteurized, raw, lactose-free, low-fat, 2%, 1%, skim, fat-free, or natural, she is sent to slaughter. There is no such thing as a slaughter-free dairy industry."

—

Ari (photo credit: Farm Sanctuary)

Ari, Bill, and Alicia

On our informative Farm Sanctuary tour, we also met Ari, Bill, and Alicia—three beautiful goats who were happy to be scratched around their horns. These three had come from a small feedlot and slaughter operation in Watsonville, California. While there is no large-scale factory farming of goat milk yet, there is cruelty in this small industry. The goats were considered "spent," as they were not producing as much milk as younger goats, even though they were just a few years old and still had much life left. They had been sold at auction for meat and ended up at this small slaughterhouse in Watsonville. Someone driving by saw a cow with a broken, bleeding horn, and called the local animal control. Animal control is not allowed to go into large factory farms, as that is USDA's territory, but they can investigate smaller facilities and often find unimaginable cruelty there. The authorities found goats that were all extremely sick, skinny, and dehydrated; as well, they had parasites and lice. They obtained a court order and were able to confiscate fifteen goats and one cow. These animals had no idea that they had just won the critter lottery and would now be pampered at the three-hundred-acre Farm Sanctuary in Orland, California. They are a few of the lucky ones, but other animals are languishing in miserable conditions on small-scale, family, free-range, cage-free farming operations all over the world. Animal control did prosecute the owner; however, he was given a minimal reprimand and continues operating as a feedlot and slaughterhouse today.

"Alternative" Egg Production

A chicken is a complex creature, with social and psychological needs beyond the basics of food and water. She needs sun to warm her feathers and earth to peck, scratch, build a nest, and dust-bathe in. She needs levels and branches to fly and perch on. She needs to be in a world of activity and stimulus. Even in "alternative" egg production, these complex needs often go unmet, and she is unable to perform basic natural behaviors. A growing number of producers now label their eggs as cage-free, yet most of these birds do not have access to the outside and are kept in large, windowless warehouses with thousands of hens crowded onto the floor. Being so overcrowded, birds will begin to peck at each other as they vie for space. A hen can live in perpetual fear of more aggressive birds. To prevent damage to the "product," the industry will remove the front portion of their beak in the same way as in standard production. The industry uses the innocuous euphemism of *beak trimming* for this cruel process. Animal advocates use a somewhat more dysphemistic term of *debeaking*, which is inaccurate to some extent, because the entire beak is not removed, just the tip. However, the pain that the animals experience is not overstated. Removal of the tip of the sensitive beak with a hot blade has been scientifically proven to cause severe acute and chronic pain.[7], [8]

Furthermore, even in cage-free and other alternative production, many chickens are forced to live in dark, filthy buildings with the horrible stench of ammonia from the buildup of their droppings and no ventilation. This toxic gas causes pain and injury to the chickens' eyes and throats and is called ammonia burn. This overwhelming smell forces workers to enter with masks and goggles. Even cage-free companies with names like Humane Harvest acquire their chicks from cruel hatcheries, debeak their chickens, send them to slaughter at only two years old, and can have up to ten thousand birds in one building with no access to the outside.[9]

All chicks born to become chicken, turkey, or duck meat, as well as those destined to be egg producers, come from hatcheries. There are no special humane hatcheries for alternative production. Hatcheries are sterile, heartless factories where baby birds are hatched in large metal drawers, with no mother hen to reassure them or soft nests to provide comfort. Baby chicks are symbols of purity, sweetness, gentleness, and love. They are often depicted on cards at Easter or for welcoming a new human baby because of their adorable appeal. It is a cruel irony that beings so helpless and fragile, so adored as a representation of lovability, would be as horrifically treated as most chicks are in animal-food production, be it at a factory farm or some alternative-label facility.

Just after they have pecked out of their shells and opened their eyes to search for their mothers, baby chicks are violently thrown on conveyer belts and roughly handled by fast-paced workers, sexing, separating, and painfully debeaking them with a hot blade at the hatchery. Male baby chicks are considered a waste product of the egg industry. They are not the breed of broiler chicken that plumps up fat fast, so they are not profitable to be raised for meat. Baby male chicks in the egg industry are killed by the millions every year. Thrown into huge grinders, they're crushed alive for fertilizer, or thrown away in plastic bags in dumpsters, where they slowly suffocate under the weight of their brothers in all extremes of weather out behind the hatcheries.[10] This is undoubtedly one of the most devastatingly cruel aspects of animal agriculture and again, it is inherent to the industry, regardless of the label.

Dr. Karen Davis of United Poultry Concerns has stated that baby birds start "talking" to their mothers while still in the egg, and the mother hen responds. Nestled in a warm nest with his brothers and sisters, he exchanges clucks and coos of comfort though the thin shell. But the heartless hatchery offers no such soothing sounds or family connection. Dr. Davis wrote, "Whenever I think of baby chicks in the mechanical incubators, hatchery mutilation rooms, filthy sheds, terrifying trucks, and slaughterhouses, I imagine the lost calls of all the birds in the world that will never be answered."[11]

In 2009, David[i] worked at the Cal-Cruz chicken and duck hatchery in Santa Cruz, California. He conducted an undercover investigation for Compassion Over Killing (COK), a nonprofit animal-protection organization. Among Cal-Cruz Hatchery's customers were farms that supplied meat to Whole Foods, an industry leader in animal welfare standards, but what David experienced was heart wrenching and far removed from any reasonable standards of welfare. Every time there is an undercover investigation, no matter the size or scale of the operation, no matter the label on the product, farmed animals all too often suffer unimaginably cruelty.

---

i This is a false name to protect his identity.

This investigator witnessed newly hatched baby chicks not strong enough to get out of the egg on their own being tossed sometimes five or six feet into buckets, rejected as not suitable to go on through production, and left to suffer. One chick is shown on video drowning in a bucket of liquid waste. David said, "There would be eggshells and muck, and the liquid waste would be collected in buckets, and live birds would be carelessly tossed in. I filmed a tiny chick struggling and drowning in a bucket of waste." The workers offered no veterinary care or pain relief to the suffering newborns. Throughout the facility were conveyer belts and metal sorters, and birds would frequently get caught in the machinery. David continued, "I documented birds that were severely injured—legs torn, wings torn from their bodies, intestines and entrails out of their bodies, the skin ripped from their bodies, all while they are still alive—suffering horribly, really gruesome injuries—and they were just left on the floor for hours." The owner was fully aware of the cruelty and ignored it, creating a culture of indifference to the misery. These are not the kind of conditions one would expect when purchasing chicken meat from Whole Foods, a company that boasts of higher standards of animal care as a marketing strategy. David also worked in a turkey hatchery. When asked if it was any better, he said no, it was worse.

COK was victorious in settling an animal cruelty lawsuit against Cal-Cruz Hatchery, and as a result of the settlement, the hatchery committed to permanent closure, never to abuse another baby bird again. Unfortunately, this is industry standard for a hatchery, and millions more newborn birds endure these conditions, labeled "humane" every day. As words can only communicate a portion of the story, please to go to the resource page at the end of this book and watch the video of this hatchery investigation.

The Animal Legal Defense Fund (ALDF) is a nonprofit organization in California that focuses on animal protection through the legal system, seeking stronger enforcement of anti-cruelty laws and filing lawsuits against animal abusers. Recently, ALDF has filed a lawsuit against Judy's Family Farm Eggs (just one brand sold under the business Petaluma Egg Farm) in the Superior Court of California for false advertising. Along with the idyllic image on the front of the carton—a chicken and her chicks freely roaming in a grassy meadow with a butterfly floating above—they state in their advertising that their hens are "raised in the wide-open spaces of Sonoma Valley, where they are free to run, scratch, and play." They also claim that "all our hens have access to the outdoors and enjoy large communal areas with natural ventilation and sunlight." However, the lawsuit was filed because, contrary to the ads, the chickens on Judy's Family Farm are tightly confined inside massive industrial sheds, with no access to the outside. They are not "free to run, scratch, and play." On the contrary, they live miserable lives, in dark warehouses where their feet never touch grass, no different than any commercial egg-laying chicken.

The company is intentionally misleading their concerned customers into believing that the animals have a good life, and they are profiting from that lie with higher prices. People who support Judy's are paying a premium for those eggs because of the promise that the chickens are happy. Judy's Family Farm Eggs has taken advantage of the kind hearts of compassionate people who are seeking out alternatives and are willing to pay more for what they have been deceived into believing are humane conditions. California has several laws that protect consumers from false claims, including the False Advertising Law and the Unfair Competition Law. ALDF is challenging Judy's Family Farm Eggs under these protective regulations, in what is sure to be a revealing case regarding alternative animal production. We are seeing more and more of these lawsuits, as producers take advantage of these unregulated labels and lie to the consumers about the quality of their product and the conditions of the animals.

Georgia (photo credit: Farm Sanctuary)

At Farm Sanctuary, we also met a few lovely little chickens, but some were limping pitifully. When we inquired about the chickens, we were told that these hens had been rescued from a small, pasture-based egg operation. When these birds were chicks, the workers had put metal identification bands on their legs. As they grew, the workers had not removed the tiny bands, and they had slowly cut into their growing legs, some down to the bone. When the chickens were rescued from this alternative operation, all of the bands had to be carefully hand-removed. For many of them, like Georgia and Luca, their little legs are still sensitive and painful where the bands sliced into the muscle and nerves. This is not the kind of care, or lack of care, consumers expect when they purchase free-range eggs.

Whether free-range, cage-free, or not, all of the hens still go to slaughter, usually before two years of age, for chicken soup and other low-quality meat products. Humane egg production in any commercial operation, alternative or otherwise, is simply a euphemism intended to deceive the consumer into spending more money; it is a complete oxymoron.

"Alternative" Meat Production

Again we find that the situation for unconventional production of meat differs very little from a standard operation. In alternative meat production, the animals are still separated from their mothers at birth, and they endure painful mutilations. Cows and steers undergo dehorning, where workers cut or burn the horns from their heads, and they receive third-degree burns from branding without painkillers. Pigs undergo agonizing castration and tooth filing, neither with pain relief. Turkeys are debeaked and detoed without anesthesia, which proves that animals are still overcrowded in sheds or mud-filled lots (otherwise there would be no need for debeaking/detoeing) and are at risk of injury from fighting. Even on free-range farms, just a few weeks after birth, chickens and turkeys can suffer from crippling bone disease due to human-induced breeding. Even standing becomes painful, and many are unable to walk or can only limp. Pigs raised for alternative pork products suffer tail docking (a procedure in which the animal's tail is amputated) and ear notching (having sections of their ears cut out for identification purposes). Some pigs with access to the outdoors have a large ring pierced though their nose so they do not root in the dirt, thus cruelly denying one of their most basic behavioral desires.[ii] Animals raised for meat usually

---

ii If the producer does not want the pigs to root, then it is likely there are too many pigs in too small an area, and the rooting will cause erosion and soil damage, as the pigs do not have enough space to spread out naturally.

don't live past their first year. These particular breeds have been genetically altered to get full-sized fast and go to slaughter before they have ever really lived. In their entire lives it is rare for them to experience all four seasons of a year.

Transportation

Most animals from "organic" or "humane" production go to the same slaughterhouses as conventionally raised animals, and they usually get there in the same way—by being transported long distances in semi-trucks. Chickens are shipped in crates where stacked cages are packed so tightly that they can barely move or even stand up straight. Cows and pigs are crammed into trucks and are forced to go without food, water, or rest for as much as three days. Animals are transported in everything from extreme heat to bitter cold, and even if they were healthy at the beginning of the trip, many reach the destination sick and some dead. They die from dehydration, exhaustion, hypothermia, or congestive heart failure from the stress. Others perish from what the industry terms "transport or shipping fever," a pneumonia-like respiratory disease from the tremendous strain of the journey.[12] Birds dying in agony and cows suffering and unable to stand are acceptable losses to this cruel industry, and there is little incentive to make their journey even slightly more pleasant with simple heating, cooling, water, and rest.

Animals being transported to slaughter routinely have food and water purposely withheld, sometimes for days, which adds difficulty to the already-arduous journey to the slaughterhouse. Food is withheld to reduce soiling of the transport trucks, to avoid wasting feed that will not have time to convert to meat and to evacuate the animals' bowels so there is a lower chance of *E. coli*, *Salmonella*, and other pathogen contamination at slaughter.[13] Fasting can be an unpleasant experience, with hunger pain, disorientation, dizziness, irritability, and stress. In *How Happy is Your Meat? Confronting (Dis)connectedness in the 'Alternative' Meat Industry*, Kathryn Gillespie sums up the terrible experience of transporting farmed animals this way: "The effects of transporting livestock include stress, bruising, trampling, suffocation, heart failure, heat stroke, sunburn, bloat, poisoning, predation, dehydration, exhaustion, injuries, and fighting."[14] Even a prisoner destined for lethal injection is afforded a last meal of his choosing, but these innocent animals who have done nothing to deserve this dreadful fate, are denied even the simple pleasure of food and a full belly in the end.

Slaughter

For meat to be legally sold in the United States, the animal must be slaughtered in a USDA-approved facility. It is cost prohibitive to have a USDA-approved slaughterhouse on most small-scale farms, so even animals from alternative and small farms are shipped, sometimes hundreds of miles, to the same slaughter facilities as animals from industrial-scale and factory farms. However, the farmer can still put the Humane label on his meat, as there is no federal regulation on the term. We will delve deeper into the specifics of labeling in the next chapter.

Most animals raised in supposedly humane conditions come to the same slaughterhouses as all the other unfortunate animals in the meat, dairy, and egg industry. An ill-fated "happy" cow can be jabbed with sticks and electric prods just as the other animals can; she can be yelled at and cussed at by the workers as she is crammed together with others in fear and trepidation of what is to come. The panic starts to spread as she hears the screams of the animals in front of her. She will hear the loud shots of the bolt gun, the sizzle and squeaks of scalding water and machinery. She doesn't want to be hurt; she doesn't want to die. She will fight the best she can and bellow out in terror as she is hoisted up by one leg, but the inevitable, awful end will come.

The bolt gun is designed to shoot four-inch rods into the animals' brains, rendering them unconscious, but an animal struggles and the assembly line moves at a rapid pace, the bolt gun will all too often miss, just causing intense pain. The animal will then go on to have his or her throat slit while fully conscious. Pete[iii], a former employee at a lamb slaughterhouse, saw horrors each excruciating day. He witnessed animals being dismembered while still fully conscious. Pete said, "I saw lambs that were crying out and still moving on their own responding to touch ten minutes after having their throats cut." Please take a moment and let this sink in. Picture a lamb, a symbol of gentleness and innocence, in severe and prolonged agony at slaughter. Most people, if they saw a lamb in pain on the side of a rural road, would feel sadness and empathy and try to gain assistance for this animal in distress. Millions of lambs are suffering behind the dark doors of the slaughterhouses—they are in no less need of assistance.

What a chicken experiences in the industrial abattoir is a painfully prolonged nightmare. Organic, free-range and other "humanely" raised chickens are carelessly thrown about by the workers and hung upside down with their ankles hooked in a moving conveyor belt. David[iv] was also employed at a chicken slaughterhouse. He worked in the "live-hang" area, taking birds from the trucks and hanging them by their feet on hooks. "You had to work really quickly, at an incredible speed, using a lot of force, so you are grabbing the birds by the hocks and slamming their feet into these shackles." David said that many of the birds' legs and feet would become injured in this process, with bruising, hemorrhaging,

---

iii This is a false name to protect his identity.

iv This is a false name to protect his identity.

and broken bones, and some of them already had leg injuries and deformities. He continued, "When I think about it, I can't get the feeling of their broken legs out of my mind. The first time you grab a chicken by the legs and expect to feel hard, solid bone, and all you feel is mush, is a horrible feeling. I've had severely broken bones in my life, and I know how painful any slight movement can be. So to be forcefully handled and shackled in that condition, that is nothing short of torture."

As they are taken though the processing, while hanging upside down, all birds—chickens, turkeys, and ducks—are first shocked with a high-voltage electrical water-bath "stunning." This painful electric shock is intended to paralyze the muscles of their feather follicles to facilitate feather release, and it is meant to immobilize them for the next stage of throat-slitting by a mechanical blade. Instead of relieving the birds' suffering, the stunning intensifies their agony with powerful electric shocks pulsing through their faces and bodies. It does not diminish the horrifically painful throat cutting, when the birds choke and gag on their own blood in what must be one of the most terrifying experiences imaginable.[15] The blood then gushes from their bodies, and it can take agonizing minutes to be rendered unconscious.[16] Some are struggling so much and attempting to free their feet with their beaks that they miss the electric shock and/or the blade altogether and are fully aware and conscious and have not bled out for the next stage of the assembly line—a terrifying dunking in a tank of scalding hot water.[17], [18] It is estimated that millions of birds go into the scalding tank completely conscious every year.[19] Virgil Butler, a former Tyson slaughterhouse worker said, "When this happens, the chickens flop, scream, kick, and their eyeballs pop out of their heads. Then, they often come out the other end with broken bones and disfigured and missing body parts, because they've struggled so much in the tank."

In 2009, the Humane Society of the United Sates (HSUS) conducted an undercover investigation at a small-scale, certified organic veal slaughterhouse in Vermont, called Bushway Packing Inc. The investigator documented newborn calves from dairy cow mothers being kicked, beaten, and stuck repeatedly with electric prods. Workers threw water on their heads and bodies so the electric shock would be more painful. The video showed calves fully conscious and kicking when they were hanging upside down by one leg, their throats slit open. At one point on the video, in front of a USDA inspector, a calf is skinned alive without his throat being slit. The calf helplessly jerks and kicks as his skin is cut away from the muscle and ripped off. The abuse was so egregious that workers pleaded guilty to felony aggravated animal cruelty and were prohibited from participating in any live animal enterprise in the future, yet these kinds of horrors continue to happen every day in slaughterhouses across the country. Words cannot tell the whole story; please see the link on our resource page to witness this investigation. Remember, this slaughterhouse was considered a small-scale, organic, "mom-and-pop" facility.

While these conditions apply equally to many animals under Humane labels, there are a tiny percentage of animals killed in ways that are widely touted as being improvements. Some of these "lucky" animals are slaughtered at one of a very few Temple Grandin-approved slaughterhouses, where they ease the panic and take them in for slaughter one by one. Or a supposedly fortunate chicken is turned upside down in a killing cone at a small farm, but still having her throat slit and choking on her blood. Perhaps the animal didn't panic as much and perhaps she didn't have the same level of fear and adrenaline as the slightly more unfortunate ones in the standard facilities. But the pain is the same, she fights for life all the same, and in the end, she is still dead. Her life was stolen, taken for no reason other than to supply the insatiable demand of our consumer choices.

In alternative meat production, the consumer is assured that these animals lived happy lives and had humane deaths, yet little is known about the difference between the slaughter methods of large industrial, factory-farms and the smaller-scale production.[20] Poultry, which constitutes 95 percent of animals slaughtered in the United States, are exempt from the Humane Methods of Livestock Slaughter Act, which states that an animal must be rendered unconscious before slaughter,[21] yet the enforcement of this law is sorely lacking as the former examples of the slaughter of lambs and calves show. The killing cone method used in alternative and small-scale slaughter for poultry is extremely cruel. Perhaps not surprisingly, throat cutting is not as quick or as painless as many believe. The bird is first frightened and disoriented by being shoved upside down in a metal or plastic cone. Her throat is then cut with a knife and her blood spurts out in a catch sink while she kicks and struggles in agony—sometimes for minutes. The throat is full of nerve endings and pain receptors; it is an extremely sensitive part of the body, for a chicken or a human. The *Australian Veterinary Journal* stated in an article on humane euthanasia, "the use of throat cutting without prior stunning must be considered an inhumane and barbaric process,"[22] yet this is the common method in both large *and* small-scale slaughter. The chicken is often still alive and panicked when she is next placed in the tank of scalding-hot water. This killing cone is the method of slaughter acceptably considered humane by alternative industry standards. As words can only express a fragment of the gruesome realities of slaughter, we encourage the reader to go to the resource section in the back of the book and learn where to find the videos.

Alameda Free Library

1550 Oak St.

Alameda, CA 94501

510-747-7777

Date: 10/4/2017

Time: 6:00:50 PM

Fines/Fees Owed: $0.00

Total Checked Out: 2

Checked Out

Title: The ultimate betrayal : is there happy
meat?
Barcode: 33341007019922
Due Date: 10/25/2017 23:59:59

Title: Thanking the monkey : rethinking the way
we treat animals
Barcode: 33341007413254
Due Date: 10/25/2017 23:59:59

Mobile Slaughter Units

To avoid the stress of transport, and perhaps the resulting economic damage to the meat that would therefore undermine profit, some small-scale farms that can afford it will incorporate slaughter on-site or utilize a recent development called a Mobile Slaughter Unit (MSU). Sometimes called a mobile meat processing unit or mobile harvester, the MSU is a USDA-certified trailer with slaughtering equipment, which comes to the farm for killing and processing. It is basically a slaughterhouse on wheels. Becoming more and more popular with small-scale agriculture operations, the MSU then brings the dead animals' bodies to a processing facility for further butchering and packaging. MSUs are intended to slaughter just a few animals. A standard thirty-six foot trailer can kill ten cows, twenty-four pigs and forty lambs in a day.[23] While it does eliminate the horrors of transport, it is important to ask whether the actual process of slaughter is more humane.

The MSU is touted as being one of the most benevolent methods of slaughtering animals. The trailer arrives at the farm with a USDA inspector, who observes the process. Larger animals are taken into a chute or small enclosure to be stunned, usually with a "captive blot gun," a high-powered gun that shoots a rod into the brain of the animal to render him unconscious; it's the very same kind that is used in a commercial slaughterhouse. The movement of the struggling animal can cause the bolt gun to miss, and sometimes it takes two or three tries to render the animal unconscious. Alternatively, they can just shoot him in the head with a firearm. The USDA's Mobile Slaughter Unit Compliance Guide states, "In most circumstances, if a firearm is used, then the head cannot be saved for edible product, except for the tongue."[24]

The animal's throat is then slit—again, just as in a standard slaughterhouse—and the animal bleeds out on a concrete pad or a patch of grass. It can take approximately five minutes for him to bleed out and die. He is then dragged into the trailer and hung for cleaning, disemboweling, and dismembering, in the same way as at a slaughterhouse. The head, feet, hide, and genitals are severed. Parts of the body that cannot be sold are left on the farm for disposal. The carcass is then cut in half, sprayed with an acid solution, and stored in the cooler section of the trailer for transport to the cut-and-wrap facility, where the meat is packaged for sale.[25]

Sizable pools of blood in the dirt or grass outside can attract flies and other insects. As in any other slaughterhouse, they must use an assortment of insecticides, fungicides, and rodenticides to discourage pests that are attracted to the smells of blood and death. However, the MSU is a very small space, where the workers and carcasses can more easily come in contact with these chemicals. As with any other slaughter operation, there are hazards that can contaminate the product in MSUs. Usual slaughter dangers are: "1) Control of feces, ingesta, or milk contamination; 2) Disease-producing microorganisms (*E. coli*, *Salmonella*); and 3) Chemical, pesticide, or drug residues."[26]

While the MSU is considered to be the least cruel of the limited alternatives to a commercial slaughterhouse, the method of slaughter is basically the same; they are held to no higher standards. In essence, an animal can have essentially the same experience with either the MSU or a larger slaughterhouse, a frightening, traumatic, and horrifying death. An animal is not going to care whether she had her throat slit in the dirt by a trailer or in a full-sized abattoir; she will fight to live and resist death to the end all the same, no matter where she is being killed.

Language of Death

Many of these alternative farms use the euphemism *harvest* instead of *slaughter* to describe killing animals. This is an obvious sugarcoating of reality as a way to soften the appalling truth. In its usual usage, the term harvest refers to the season of autumn when crops are cut and reaped. Animals have no season and can be killed at any time, so it is a misnomer to use the euphemistic term *harvest* to portray their deaths.

Also, there is no correlation between the way that animals experience emotional, psychological, and physical pain and the experience of plants during the agricultural process. We would not say we are going out to slaughter the broccoli. The terms are not interchangeable. Broccoli does not have any behavioral indicators that it experiences pain. It does not scream out in trepidation, struggle to get away, or have any of the same physiological or physiological capacities that would cause it to feel trauma in any way that is remotely similar to what an animal feels. We know through observation of behavior that animals have the capacity to suffer and feel pain. It is the same way we know a baby feels pain. Pain is a lower-brain-stem function that all animals, including fish, equally possess. According to current scientific knowledge, all animals that possess a central nervous system feel pain in a similar way. A cow, chicken, or fish can suffer just as much as a dog or a human. Unlike plants, animals scream when in pain; they thrash and fight to avoid oppression. Some will argue that plants do feel pain. This assertion is neither scientifically proven nor anecdotally verifiable. But even if this were the case, a plant-based diet would *still* cause the least amount of suffering. If you eat animal products, you are actually killing more plants, because the animals who are being slaughtered have eaten an excess of plants, thus killing more plant-life than if you just ate plants directly.

The words harvest and slaughter are not transposable. This is nothing more than a euphemistic soft-pedaling of a violent reality that no one wants to think about or feel that they have contributed to.

Raised With Care?

Niman Ranch is touted as one of the most humane and most sustainable farms for meat and eggs in the United States. It sells more than thirty-three million pounds of alternative meat annually.[27] On its logo it states, Raised with Care. The ranch's former owner and namesake, Bill Niman, was pushed out of his own operation because the shareholders wanted to lower standards while maintaining the same prices—at the cost of the animals' welfare. Mr. Niman has lamented that he no longer eats Niman Ranch meats.[28]

But before all this, his wife, Nicolette Niman, a vegetarian and author of *The Righteous Porkchop*, a book about meat consumption beyond factory farms, worked with Temple Grandin to ensure that the animals from the over 650 participating farms are raised outdoors, stay with their family groups (with exceptions), and are able to express their natural behaviors (to a certain degree). These small farmers agree to adhere to certain protocols of treatment and processing of animals. Special attention is paid to their feed, assuring "cattle will never receive feeds or supplements containing any fish, animal or meat by-products (including feather meal), fecal material, or garbage," the standard fare for regular production, although cow's milk products are allowed to be fed to the pigs and lambs.

They say in their cattle-handling protocols, "At all times, humane handling will be practiced." However, there seems to be a disconnection between their values and their practices, as electric prods are allowed, and there is no pain relief required for castration or tail docking. Castration can be performed in the same horrific method as at any commercial farm, simply by cutting with a knife causing the baby animals to writhe and scream in pain or by wrapping a tight band just above the testes, cutting off the blood supply, and then waiting for days or weeks for them to fall off—a long and painful process.

For electric prods, this is what is said in the Niman Ranch cattle protocols as of January 10, 2011.

Electric prods ... can, if necessary, be used for three things:

1. An animal won't go into the squeeze chute.

2. An animal is down in the squeeze chute.

3. An animal is down at a truck step.

A "down" animal is an animal who has either lain down or fallen down and can't, or won't, get up for some reason—usually because they are sick, injured, or in pain. Even a small "hot-shot" device that fits in a pocket can generate up to 4,500 volts of electricity.[29] To apply an electric prod to a downed animal is extremely cruel and is using excessive force and fear to coerce the animal to move. This certainly does not sound like "humane handling."

In their hog protocols, again, Niman Ranch does not state a requirement of pain reduction medication for castration. Castration in hog production is necessary, as an unaltered male's meat will not be as desirable a product; it will have what is called boar taint. All males must be castrated for the meat to be sellable, and castration can be an excruciating procedure with or without anesthesia.[30, 31] The only mention of sustainability in the protocols consists of the statement, "Niman Ranch expects certified farmers to raise hogs in an environmentally safe and approved manner that adheres to all county, state, and federal standards"—yet no details are given of what that would require. Just saying they adhere to the standards is weak at best. It is apparent that the standards are far from adequate to protect the environment from hog waste polluting our nation's waterways.[32] This is a large part of the reason people are seeking labels like Niman Ranch; they want a higher set of standards, yet there is very little, if any, difference from a standard operation.

In the Niman Ranch protocols for lambs it states that "tail docking and castration must be performed prior to one month of age." There is no mention of how that should be done or of a requirement for anesthesia. Tail docking is a painful procedure whereby the tail of the animal is cut off to a stub, with about an inch or two remaining. Niman Ranch lambs, while just babies less than a month old, are castrated and have their tails cut off without painkillers. This violent mutilation is the standard practice of what is widely considered the most humane product available.

In their cage-free egg protocols, there is no prohibition against the debeaking of hens. Since this is an industry standard practice, and given their lenience with tail docking and castration, it is logical to assume that many, if not all, of the hens that are Niman approved have undergone this painful procedure. This practice has the potential to cause continuous pain and chronic problems for the birds, including the inability to eat normally. Debeaking is far from a humane practice, and the fact that Niman Ranch does not disapprove of this practice, as well as allowing tail docking and castration, shows that even they are putting profit before principle.

You simply cannot provide the quantity of meat or eggs needed to feed the world, and make a profit, with humanely treated animals. It is economically impossible.

Ruby (photo credit: Animal Place)

Ruby

Ruby was big—really big. Her floppy ears fell over her eyes and pointed down to her wiggling round snout as she munched on some grass. It is hard to believe that this gigantic pig was once the runt of the litter. Ruby came from a small pasture-based farm that advertised an idyllic life for their animals. The farm is open to the public and even gives tours, a very rare practice even among alternative farms. This makes it all the more shocking that, just as on a large, conventional farm, the runts were being brutally killed. Runts, the smallest piglets of a litter, may not grow to be a profitable size, so in many agricultural schools and hog operations it is considered a waste of feed to let them live. They are killed by starvation or by what is called "thumping"— throwing them violently to the ground or against the wall.

Thumping was to be the fate of Ruby the runt, before she had a name. A visitor on a tour was horrified to learn that she would be killed in such a violent manner and begged to take her. Ruby won the pig lottery and ended up at Animal Place. She now shares her acres with other pig friends under the blue skies of Grass Valley, California, blissfully unaware of the brutal fate that could have been hers.

While it may be possible for some smaller operations to allow for what might be considered humane living circumstances (excepting the slaughter, which obviously cannot be considered humane under any circumstances), as demand increases and humane operations increase in size, they will inevitably have to compromise their seemingly benevolent standards, just as Niman Ranch did. It is important to note that providing any financial support in the form of consumer dollars to livestock agriculture can be a slippery slope. While it may be possible for smaller operations to offer a bit more space and a slightly more comfortable existence, as demand and competition increases and alternative operations increase in size, the profit motive provides a powerful incentive for farmers to cut costs by decreasing living space and being less cautious about how the animals are treated in general. It is an unavoidable law of economics that to maximize profit you must increase the efficiency of production. In livestock production, this usually means less land to roam on, less consideration to the health of the animals, and shorter life spans, all of which are antithetical to the humane label.

This is especially true if a producer has a competitor who is able to sell products at a lower price because he has spent less money on food, care, and land. This is what brought us to industrial factory farming in the first place: competition and efficiency.

Let's not forget that small farms exist for the same reasons that big industrial animal agriculture does—to raise, kill, and sell animals; essentially, they are in business to make a profit. Large-scale operations are the drivers of animal agriculture because they are more efficient and are better at maximizing profits. As much as we may have a romanticize image of rustic ranchers, all operations have to remain competitive, and to survive in a competitive market, the business must always consider respect for the welfare of animals to be secondary. Behind the marketing images on the alternative farming websites of rolling pastures and cute pink piglets, there are the cold realities of economics and business. When the welfare of animals contradicts the bottom line, as it inevitably and inescapably does, it is the animals who suffer and the producers who profit.

The alternative animal-product industry is just a niche market now, so suppliers can enjoy high demand with a restricted supply and therefore use the hollow promise of treating the animals a little bit better as a ploy to charge higher prices. But as demand increases, and more ranchers get on the alternative bandwagon, producers need to become more efficient, more fugal, and more competitive. It is the animals who pay for the efficiency of production. Living, sentient beings cannot be bought and sold as commodities with any realistic expectation of truly humane treatment. Our own species' history is a tragic lesson in this certainty. In a for-profit business, values and morals will be compromised when profitability is threatened. Vasile Stanescu, co-senior editor of the *Critical Animal Studies* book series at Stanford University said, "Whenever profit and animal welfare contradict, it is the profit consideration which always trumps." In the end, after all, it is a business.

There is a mutualistic relationship between "alternative/humane" operations and more mainstream companies; to support any aspect of the animal industry with consumer dollars usually means that you are supporting other more inhumane aspects of the industry as well. Keep in mind that all aspects of animal industry, from small/ organic/local/humane to industrial/large/corporate/factory farms, share resources, technology, and professionals from the service sector, such as hatcheries, veterinarians, workers, technicians, transportation, slaughterhouses, etc. Humane/Organic/Local and other feel-good labels purchase much of the same machinery and services as mainstream industrial factory farming does. When you spend your consumer dollars on even the most seemingly ethical livestock products, a portion of that money goes to fund the same pillar industries that support factory farming as well. As principled people who would go as far as possible to not support the abuses described herein, consumers should not support *any* part of the livestock industry.

Finally, it is unnecessary to kill animals for our consumption as food. The millions of vegans around the world are living proof of this. So why contribute to the bloodshed? Why attempt to assuage our consciences with this feel-good cover-up of humane slaughter? Happy meat? Killing is killing. There is no label that will change that. Like human animals, nonhuman animals want to forage and eat, enjoy the sun on their bodies, have babies, rest, play, and take pleasure from life. We have no right to take that from them, especially when we live healthier and longer when we don't consume their flesh. Our individual and collective happiness largely depends on our meaningful relationships with others. We should include animals under that rubric; then, being conscious of animal suffering and abstaining from our individual complicity in their deaths could be a source of great happiness. Living a compassionate lifestyle provides us with a sense of meaning when we realize that our lives can be true expressions of kindness and peace. Consuming animal products, alternative or not, is antithetical to our higher standards of ethical conduct as a means to individual and collective happiness. Embrace a new, compassionate commitment to an active and meaningful sense of kindness through a plant-based diet. In this way, our lives will be an expression of true humanity, altruism, and caring toward all living beings.

Chapter 3
Labels: What's the Buzz?

You must remember, my dear lady, the most important rule of any successful illusion: First, the people must want to believe in it.

— Libba Bray, *The Sweet Far Thing*

It's easier to fool people than to convince them they have been fooled.

—Mark Twain

Let's now take a closer look at the new feel-good buzzword labeling of alternative animal products and what these terms really mean. This new terminology has little or no regulatory oversight and is lulling consumers into a false sense that the industry is rigorously regulated and scrutinized for compliance. Trusting consumers assume that the labels actually mean that there is a significant difference between the labeled product and those from conventional agriculture. This is not always the case. This chapter will reveal that there is often no legitimacy or accuracy to the slogans used in labeling animal products. It is unfortunate that we live in a world where we cannot trust the tag lines that the industry feeds us; mass deception has forced the informed consumer to live in suspicion. Some operations are a bit better, but better is far from ideal. Producers are systematically betraying consumers' trust. This chapter assesses claims specifically designed to promote the idea that a certain product is produced with consideration for the well-being of the animals. We will explore the environmental impact claims of alternative animal production in chapter 6.

The United States Department of Agriculture (USDA) and, in some cases, the Food and Drug Administration (FDA) are the agencies responsible for food product labeling and marketing claims. Animal care labels, such as Free Range and Grass Fed, currently have no regulatory definitions, so the USDA uses unofficial, subjective descriptions as guidelines. Only Third Party Certified labels, including Organic and Certified Humane, have actual on-site inspection for compliance. All the other labels can be obtained with just the testimony of the farm owner or manager, with no inspection or oversight from regulatory agencies. All a producer needs to do is fill out a form, say whatever he wants, and the label is awarded.[1, 2] This is an example of regulation in its weakest possible form, and producers take opportunistic advantage of the flimsy supervision.

In fact, the oversight is so lax that even operations like Hudson Valley Farms, the United States' exclusive producer of foie gras, uses the Humanely Raised label. Foie gras is the controversial cuisine made by shoving a thick metal pipe down a duck's throat and forcing down food to grossly engorge his liver up to eight times its normal size for consumption as an expensive delicacy. Foie gras production universally ranks as one of the cruelest forms of animal agriculture, and public outrage at this inhumane practice has resulted in bans of the product in Denmark, Finland, Germany,

Luxembourg, Israel, Norway, Poland, Sweden, Switzerland, the United Kingdom, and the Czech Republic, with the state of California recently joining the ranks of places that forbid this cruel practice. Undercover animal protection investigators confirmed the cruelty in foie gras production firsthand after witnessing ducks physically debilitated and unable to stand or walk as they painfully suffered from liver disease and organ rupture. It is an outrage that Hudson Valley is able to say their foie gras is "the humane choice." Luckily, the Animal Legal Defense Fund (ALDF), a nonprofit collection of compassionate lawyers, is not going to let them get away with it. The ALDF is suing Hudson Valley for false advertising. This is a classic example of how meaningless the alternative labeling is and how little oversight is enforced on those using these descriptions. Let's take a look at some of the most prevalent labels and what they really mean.

Free Range or Pasture Raised

Before industrial animal agriculture, if an animal was *free range* or *free roaming*, this generally referred to cattle who were self-sustaining on the range, foraging for their own food and water, not requiring human-created shelter or feeding, and basically living a free life in outdoor, open spaces until roundup and slaughter. The meaning of this term has shifted in the modern age and few consumers would be able to define it now. Many would say the implication is that animals have an outdoor space to roam, which is often not the case.

Except for poultry, there are no federal guidelines or regulations for any animal to be labeled free-range in the United States. In free-range poultry production the USDA requires that "producers must demonstrate to the Agency that the poultry has been allowed access to the outside"; however, how large a space for how many birds or how long the access is given are not specified.[3] This "access" could be a door in a huge building where thousands of birds reside that is open only part of the day or certain times of the week. The outdoor area provided is often unappealing and difficult to access for all the animals, without adequate space, forage, and/or protection from predators. If there is the ability to go outside, the area can be nothing but a small five-by-five-foot square of gravel or concrete for the tens of thousands of birds crammed into a windowless warehouse—and still the farmer is able to use the feel-good USDA label of Free Range. Being flock animals, hens in so-called free-range systems are often too afraid to venture outside, in part because they lack protection from roosters or cockerels and want to stay with the safety of the flock. If the entire flock cannot go outside, then an individual will often not feel safe to do so.[4]

Because birds being raised for meat are slaughtered at such a young age, (usually at just four to six weeks old) if they were born in the autumn or winter, or during a particularly rainy spring, they will never experience the outdoors. Producers will deny the birds' access to the outside due to the weather. To award the Free Range label, the USDA relies solely on the producer's reports; there is no independent, on-site verification of their testimony.[5, 6, 7]

Turkeys are another bird on which we see these labels. Free Range and Heritage Breed labels are often applied to their deceased and dismembered body parts. A heritage breed turkey is simply a breed of turkey that is rarely used in modern animal agriculture for practical reasons. Humans prefer white breast meat, so the Broad Breasted White is now almost exclusively used. A heritage breed bird usually has more dark meat, and some can breed on their own. The Broad Breasted White, the turkey breed raised for 99 percent of the market, can no longer reproduce naturally, because it has been bred to be so huge in the breast area that a male would crush a female if he attempted to mate with her. The genders must be separated at all times, and hens are artificially inseminated. The Heritage Breed label has nothing to do with the conditions in which the bird was raised or how it was killed; it only tells us the species of the bird.

While most free-range turkey operations do offer outdoor living space, similar overcrowding to indoor environments is common. Having thousands of birds in one small area causes unnatural behaviors; they will peck and scratch at one another for space and be unable to escape injury with the tight conditions. Painful debeaking and detoeing (cutting off one or two digits of all the toes) are often still performed. The flip side of the romanticized notion of animals' free-ranging outside is that in harsh weather— cold winters and heavy rain, sleet, or snow—these operations may not have adequate indoor space for the turkeys to get out of the weather. In nature, wild turkeys would seek out protection under trees, brush, or natural slopes in the terrain, but they are unable to do so when thousands of them are confined in a muddy outdoor pen. These outfits do not provide for the turkey's complex needs or natural expression, and the result is often a miserable life.

Dakota (photo credit: Animal Place)

Dakota and Miwok

At Animal Place, we also met a gaggle of very vocal turkeys, who gobbled and chuckled at our intrusion into their barn space. Our guide, Marji, explained that they were from a California free-range turkey farm and had been dropped off at Animal Place one Thanksgiving. Dakota and Miwok were puffing up their beautiful arc of white feathers for us, and their snoods and wattles (flaps of skin hanging from the beak and neck) changed from a brilliant blue to dazzling red. This rainbow effect around the turkey's face is an amazing talent and can be an indicator of their mood.

Although it was a free-range farm they had come from, there were around twenty thousand birds in a small outdoor area.

Because of overcrowding and the fighting that can result, they were debeaked. Marji explains. "A large portion of their nerve-sensitive, blood-rich beak is cut off, and that causes lifelong pain and suffering. They are constantly feeling the loss of that missing appendage. They use their beaks to preen, to groom, to peck, to eat." These free-range birds were also detoed. Our tour guide said, "The workers go so fast and sometimes miss, so some birds have some of their toes on a foot but not others." This process is incredibly painful and can cause problems with balance and walking. Marji continued, "These guys can't mate normally, they can't fly, they can't perch—they can't do anything that a turkey naturally wants to do because they are bred to have this big breast muscle that people like to eat. Even the free-range birds are debeaked, detoed; they have that nice label that people feel good about, but they are killed when they are just four months old, when they are just babies."

All broilers (chickens raised for their meat), egg-laying hens, and turkeys—factory farmed, free-range, or organic, irrespective of labeling—come from cruel hatcheries, where they are born in metal drawers, never to have a mother hen's love and attention. They live in overcrowded conditions and are sent to the same frightening slaughterhouse as any conventional bird. Basically, when you buy "free-range" turkey, chicken meat, or eggs, that bird came from the same hatchery and went to the same slaughterhouse as any other bird, and likely had a similarly wretched life in between.

Grass Fed

When we think of grass-fed beef and other meat, we assume that the animals were pasture raised, living their whole lives in a pristine pasture, gracefully grazing on their natural diet of grass. However, in most grass-fed operations, the animals are grazed for only a few months of the year. Depending on the location and weather conditions, most are confined and fed cut grass and other forage the rest of the year.

As the term is currently defined, Grass Fed has even less impact on animal welfare than Free Range. The only regulation on this label is that the cow be fed 80 percent of his or her diet in grass; the last few months of life are often spent in feedlots, fattening up on corn. So a grass-fed cow could be confined in a barn or languish in a feedlot, caked in mud and feces, and not see growing grass beneath her hooves for months before her slaughter. The Grass Fed label has no bearing on what the cow is given other than the food, so grass-fed beef can have hormones, antibiotics, and other pharmaceutics if it is not organic. And again, it is only regulated by the farm operator's written statement; there is no on-site inspection of any kind.[8]

Humane or Humanely Raised

There is no definition or regulation on the term Humane, so this label is completely open for interpretation at the whim of the producer. Of course, what the consumer would logically think is that the animal was treated humanely throughout his or her life and into slaughter, but as revealed in the previous chapter, inherent cruelties flourish in animal agriculture. But at least the animals were treated somewhat better, right? In many situations that is not the case, as we see with the Humane Society of the United States' (HSUS) class-action lawsuit against the United States' third-largest chicken producer, Perdue™. Maryland-based Perdue™ markets their Perdue™ and Harvestland™ chicken meat as Humanely Raised on the product label and on their promotional materials.

The HSUS alleges that this is false and illegal and violates the New Jersey Consumer Fraud Act, as Perdue's method of raising and slaughtering these chickens is no different than any other factory farm where most reasonable people would find the conditions and treatment unacceptable and appalling. Playing on growing customer concern and demand for humane treatment of animals, Perdue is unethically stamping a Humane approval label on factory-farmed animal products. Perdue says they follow the standard National Chicken Council's Animal Welfare Guidelines that Temple Grandin, an expert on farmed animal handling and slaughter, calls negligent. Grandin said, "The National Chicken Council Animal Welfare Audit has a scoring system that is so lax that it allows plants or farms with really bad practices to pass." Perdue's chickens endure overcrowding in filthy warehouses, inhumane handling, transport in weather extremes without food and water for days, and the horrors of the conventional slaughterhouse, yet still they are able to label their products as humanely raised. This label is both meaningless and intentionally deceptive.

Another example comes from a lawsuit filed by Mercy for Animals (MFA) against Sparboe Farms, the fifth-largest producer of eggs, with facilities in Minnesota, Iowa, and Colorado. The suit intends to expose their false and misleading advertising. Sparboe Farms claims that animals in their care experience "the five freedoms"— no hunger, discomfort, injury, disease, or distress—and that they are able to express normal behavior. They say on their website, "At Sparboe Farms, we follow a code of conduct that *ensures* our hens receive these five essential freedoms." Yet MFA conducted two undercover investigations at Sparboe plants and found severely injured birds, unable to walk; dead, decaying carcasses in cages with live birds; baby chicks thrown into plastic bags and left to suffocate; and all the hens suffering in barren battery cages where they could barely move. These are arguably the most inhumane animal husbandry practices in modern animal agriculture. What the investigation exposed was so egregious that the FDA cited Sparboe for thirteen serious violations of food-safety laws. Basically, this was the worst-of-the-worst factory farming, but the company was making lofty claims in their promotional materials about humane treatment of their animals—all were absolute lies. Producers can say whatever they want to in order to deceive and reassure the customer and to sell products. There is no regulation or oversight stopping them.

Cage-Free

The standard practice for the egg industry is to raise hens in battery cages, rows and rows of small cages, with birds crammed inside, stacked on top of each other to fill a warehouse-sized space. Each hen has a space less than the size of a sheet of paper on which to live. She is unable to move or spread her wings; it would be the equivalent of living your entire life in a crowded elevator. This system is so cruel that exposure of the practice has garnered widespread public sympathy and starting in the United Kingdom and now affecting many US states, legislative bans on barren battery cages are being increasingly supported by the public and by legislators.[9]

This is a positive step in a compassionate direction, because it alleviates at least some modicum of suffering for the animals. But perhaps more importantly, widespread legislation is accompanied by substantial public education campaigns that expose consumers to farmed-animal suffering. This causes a shift in the public perception and popularizes the notion that farmed animals are entitled to some degree of protection against the infringement of their well-being. While these legislative reforms are essential to bring much-needed widespread education about the plight of farmed animals to the public, and being out of a cage is a significant improvement, it is unfortunate that the alternatives to intensive confinement are a variety of "cage-free" systems that still entail much animal suffering.

A cage-free operation is generally a large, windowless warehouse where tens of thousands of birds are confined inside on the floor. They endure overcrowding, with just about one square foot of floor space per bird—double what battery hens endure, but still crowded. The extreme housing density can cause some of the same problems experienced in barren battery cages, so the hens will be painfully debeaked to protect each other from pecking. While it is true that they are not in cages, a producer does not have to offer access to the outside to obtain this label. Cage-free facilities provide nesting boxes in which to lay their eggs, and some have levels, perches, or litter to dust-bathe in, offering some resemblance to nature. But all cage-free chickens come from cruel hatcheries and do not get a retirement plan. They go to a sickening slaughter when their egg production declines. They live lives of miserable confinement followed by untimely death—like almost every other hen used in food production.[10, 11]

Surprisingly, most cage-free systems are located on the same factory farms as the battery-cage operations. A company will have several large sheds on the same property. One building will be packed with hens crammed in battery cages, and the building right next to it will be cage-free, with thousands of birds on the floor. The producer is not raising the hens cage-free out of concern for the birds' welfare or because they want to be more humane. If that were the case, they would have *all* of the birds out of cages. The business has both of these systems in place to appeal to a broader customer base, offering a variety of products to make their operation more profitable. They know that there are some people who will pay more for the Cage-Free label, being under the assumption that the animal has had a happy life—but this is simply not the case.

Pete[i] was an undercover investigator who worked at three separate California egg facilities. At two of them there were both caged and cage-free buildings. The cage-free operations had an average of thirty thousand hens per dark, windowless building. Pete told us that none of the birds received any veterinary care at any of the businesses that he investigated. "So you have a bird that's dying somewhere, and you don't treat her. Someone might pick the bird up and throw her either into a trash can or outside the pen area, on the floor in the maintenance room." Pete continued, "You may pull her neck or swing her around by the head to kill her. Or you just dump them somewhere, and if they are still alive, you leave them to suffer and die." On one occasion, Pete was driving outside the cage-free building, when "I saw a cart with a bunch of dead bodies piled in it, and right on top of the pile was a live hen; it seemed that she couldn't stand. All I know is that she was sitting there with her head up on top of the pile of dead bodies. It was near the pit where they would chuck all the birds that had died, so I can only assume that she was chucked in alive."

Pete also spoke of a practice at both cage-free facilities that the workers called "scaring the birds up." These barns had hutches a few feet off the floor for the hens to lay their eggs. They preferred it when the hens laid the eggs in the boxes, so the eggs didn't crack or get squashed on the floor. The birds laid most of their eggs early in the morning, so in the evening, the workers would "scare them up." Pete explained, "We would all go in and shut the lights off and workers grabbed chickens by wings, by a leg, by anything, and just start throwing them—chucking them hard and throwing

---

i This is a false name to protect his identity.

them at the hutches. We would do it every night, so after about a week the birds learned that when the lights go off, you better go up in the hutch, or someone is going to grab you and throw you." Pete said that this kind of fear tactic was common in all the places he worked, from large factory farms to small family farms. They coerced the animals into doing what they wanted with fear and violence. The animals reacted to any human with trepidation and anxiety. The label of cage-free is exactly what it says: the birds are not in cages. It does not mean, however, that the chickens are happy or have any semblance of a good life. Their entire lives are characterized by nothing but violence and fear inflicted by their human captors.

Local

A Local label generally refers to the distance that a food has traveled to get to the market. There is certainly no consensus as to what that distance, often called food miles, must be to warrant the label. Some say that, from farm to store, a product defined as local can have traveled no more than one hundred miles, but some say up to five hundred miles. Some say as long as it was within the same state. Whole Foods Market, a chain of natural foods supermarkets, defines their Local label as meaning food that has not traveled more than seven hours by truck.

It is important to realize that even factory farms are local to somebody. We live in Sonoma County, California, home of the ever-quirky Clover Dairy. If you have ever seen their advertising, love it or hate it, you have to admit it is unique. The cartoon Clover the Cow features idiosyncratic word play from every aspect of North American culture, from movies to fairy tales, and relates them to milk production, with excessive use of the word *udder*. In the last couple of years, they have erected billboards in high-traffic areas, asking potential customers to "Support your local cow!"

So, what do people assume when they think that the cow, and therefore her milk, is local? They assume it is from a small-scale or family farm, so the cow is treated better, with some attention to her physical and emotional needs. However, Clover Dairy, as they proudly claim on their home page, supplies milk to *millions* of people throughout California, Arizona, and Nevada each day.[12] It is hardly a small-scale operation. In fact, Clover Dairy is one of the largest factory-farming dairy companies in Northern California, where the cows are overcrowded and kept pregnant by artificial insemination. The babies are stolen from their mothers at birth and sent to auction for veal or other meat. Cows are prodded into a milking room several times a day and are denied the desire to care for all the calves that they have given birth to. The cows are slaughtered for ground beef when their milk output begins to decline at less than a quarter of their natural lifespan.[13] This is what Clover Dairy is able to call a local operation, and this is more or less what one can expect from many local operations.

Somehow, the term *local* has become so synonymous with *good*, *humane*, and *environmentally friendly* that consumers feel they can stop thinking about the product beyond the label. People have been led to believe that if a product is local then it must be good, period. This becomes a distortion of basic moral considerations when consumers' critical thinking becomes so pacified by this feel-good, misleading label that they neglect to take other factors—such as animal suffering, environmental impact, or health—into consideration. Local means it was produced locally, nothing more. It does not necessarily mean that the ingredients are local, just the company. Jars of coconut oil are sold in Northern California health-food stores and are labeled as local. This label has absolutely nothing to do with how an animal was raised, fed, kept, or slaughtered—or any other significantly more important aspect of production.

Basically, the unwarranted reverence for the term *local* has enabled a brilliant marketing ploy by the agricultural industry. First, we are led to believe that a product is good if it is local, because when we buy that product we are supporting smaller-scale operations instead of corporate conglomerates. This is the first faulty assumption. Secondly, we are led to believe that these supposedly smaller-scale operations, by their very nature, are friendlier to the environment, also a fallacious assumption. Third, we are led to believe that the money stays in the community and that something local is better for the economy. Upon further exploration, in many situations, none of these assumptions are found to be true.[14]

Once the consumer has made all of these fallacious associations about the Local label, they are then manipulated into forgetting the important principles that made them value local products in the first place. Industry markets the Local label incessantly, constantly repeating its importance, and soon the consumer forgets to consider environment, worker conditions, animal exploitation, and economic considerations, and becomes essentially trained to revere the "local" consideration above everything else.

It's not that purchasing local is bad. Local consumption is neither good nor bad; it largely lacks any real relevance as to the ethical status of purchasing a certain product. If a local product meets the above criteria (i.e., low environmental impact, no animal exploitation, etc.) and is better than a nonlocal option, then by all means, please choose the local product. However, it is important to realize that there are many examples where the nonlocal product will be a better purchase when gauged by the above criteria.

Another more disturbing development that is a by-product of the reverence for local food is the know-your-butcher trend. People are led to believe that if they know the person that raised the animal or butchered him then its okay to eat his body. This may represent some small degree of progress, because consumers want a closer connection to the food that they are eating, but the pig is just as involved as the farmer, actually, much more so, for the pig gives his very life to the production process. So the pig should be afforded just as much—or even more—consideration as the farmer, who stands to profit. Maybe it would be better to get to know the pig—but then killing him would be more difficult. This trend of killing your own and backyard slaughter hobbyists is growing, and we hope that it will ultimately help people to see the moral conundrum in killing animals for food. We will be exploring this subject in more detail in chapter 4.

Family Secrets

Driving among the emerald hills of Sonoma County, California, you can hear a radio commercial claim, "Ninety-nine percent of California farms are family farms." This is probably a factually correct statement, as the owners of these farms are married and perhaps have children. But it does not necessarily follow that they are small, sustainable operations. Again, there is no legal definition for this label, and many of these so-called family farms are large, industrial, polluting agribusinesses. But even the small-scale operations, where the family is living and working on the farm, do not offer any guarantee that the animals will be well cared for or treated with kindness and respect.

Pete, who was employed at the cage-free egg facilities mentioned earlier, also worked at two dairies. One was a family-run, small-scale dairy with only two hundred cows. Compared to a factory-farmed dairy that can have as many as sixty thousand cows at a time, this was a very small operation. The owner lived and worked on the property, where the cows were free to roam in a large pasture and were primarily grass fed. Sounds like a model family farm, right? Yet on this seemingly ideal dairy farm near Twin

Falls, Idaho, Pete said, "There was a culture of abuse, including beating the hell out of cows."

On a daily basis, the workers, from the owner on down, would punch the cows with their fists, kick them with their boots, and hit them with random objects like a "big plastic cane." Pete continued, "Workers would get frustrated and punch calves in the face for not suckling the bottle and stuff. This is the same abuse that I saw on a ranch raising calves for the dairy industry in Texas: neglecting the dying, that kind of thing. It was sadistic abuse, beating the hell out of cows out of frustration and doing it when it was unnecessary and wouldn't help."

When asked why this culture of violence is so pervasive in raising farmed animals, he elaborated with this:

"Part of the problem—and this is something that no one will ever admit, but I have seen this at every farm and slaughterhouse I've worked at—is that you get people that just get frustrated, and they get upset, and they are pressured, and have to do a certain job that is oftentimes physically impossible to do it the way they are supposed to do it, and they take it out on the animals. Most of the people, when you meet them and you interact with them, they are very good, decent people. They might have a family. But over enough time and with enough pressure it seems to them there is no other way to do what they need to; they turn to violence. And a surprising amount of people do it."

Pete also worked at a family-owned pork producer. At this farm, three family members were working the farm with about four thousand breeding hogs in gestation crates, tiny cages just larger than their bodies. The pigs were unable to turn around or even lie down comfortably. At any given time, scores of sows were sick or injured and "they would let all the animals kind of linger in pens to die." At one point, there were so many hurt and sick animals, Pete said, "Everyone had to drag the crippled pigs out with catch poles around their legs, because they couldn't walk—some had broken legs—and drop them off a four-foot ledge to an area with the front loader tractor. Then they would tie a chain around their necks and hoist them up to strangle them and it would take about four or five minutes for them to stop struggling." These mother pigs were tortured to death by hanging, after weeks or months of misery from sickness and injury. The pork from this farm could easily have been labeled as coming from a small family farm.

We all know that family members can be hostile and unkind. There is a culture of violence that is pervasive throughout animal agriculture. It is accepted and common to handle farmed animals through coercion, intimidation, and cruelty. Just because an operation is small and family owned, this does not mean that they are exempt from this culture and that the animals there are happy. Family Farm is just another deceptive label to sell products to an unsuspecting public that is endeavoring to make ethical choices.

Natural or All Natural

The term *natural* refers only to what is added to the cut of meat after the animal is dead. Meat can be labeled Natural if it has no artificial colors, dyes, salts, or preservatives added. The term natural has nothing to do with the way the animal was treated, raised, housed, slaughtered, or what he was fed. "Natural" animal products could come from an animal in the intensive confinement of a factory farm; fed a diet of manure, fish meal, garbage, additives, antibiotics, and hormones; and slaughtered the same as any commercial animal. This is by far the weakest of all labels and has no bearing whatsoever on animal welfare.[15, 16]

Third Party Certified

There are a few agencies that often work with animal welfare organizations and offer certifications that go beyond the USDA regulations in terms of animal care and well-being. The most prominent of these programs are the Certified Organic and Certified Humane. These labels advertize a better life for the animals, but as we have shown, egregious practices still remain and are inherent to the industry.

Certified Organic

Gaining organic certification for animal products is a multi-year process of annual inspections with an adherence to certain rules. These mainly include avoiding a long list of chemical fertilizers in the grain fed to the animals, as well as avoiding antibiotics, vaccines, and other medications. Just over one thousand certified organic farmers raise about 2 percent of the country's total egg-laying hens, 2 percent of the total dairy cows, and less than 1 percent of the total number of cattle, pigs, and poultry in the country. Although this is a small percentage of the animal products sold today, the USDA's Economic Research Service (ERS) called organic meat "one of the fastest growing sectors in the organic industry, with total retail sales having increased by a factor of 46 between 1997 and 2007."[17]

Organic is probably the most stringent of the alternative labels with respect to environmental considerations. However, there is little difference between organic and conventional farming with respect to the animals' experience in the process of production.[18, 19] Organic labeling is regulated by the USDA, but there are also more rigorous state certification options as well. The National Organic Program federal standard applies to all farmed animal species at once; it does not address each species of animals' specific needs.

These regulations do not include minimum space allowances and do nothing to address critical aspects of animal suffering in agriculture, such as weaning, forced molting, debeaking, tail docking, ear notching, electric prod use, euthanasia, transport, hatcheries, or slaughter.[20]

To have his product labeled Organic, the farmer must refrain from using most synthetic fertilizers and pesticides on the crops that are fed to the animals. Irradiation, pharmaceuticals, and genetic engineering are also prohibited, and the animals must have "access to the outdoors." However, we see the same vague enforcement as with the free-range poultry label. This access to the outdoors may be no more than an open door to an unappealing concrete floor, out of which animals may perhaps peer but do not dare venture.[21] This inadequate concession allows the producer to proclaim that the animals have access to the outdoors, even though they never step a foot outside. John Robbins, a leading authority on animal agriculture and author of numerous books, writes in his latest book, *No Happy Cows* that "just because eggs are 'organic' doesn't mean that they are humanely raised. In fact, there are 'organic' factory-farm operations with more than eighty thousand 'organic' hens in a single building."

A study that compared organic and conventional sheep farming found no significant difference in the welfare of the animals. They compared animal dirtiness, hoof overgrowth, lameness, lesions, longevity, and mutilations such as de-horning and tail docking (cutting), but found no dissimilarity in the conditions and well-being of the sheep.[22] They did not examine the possibly greater psychological violations of separating mothers from lambs and the horrors of slaughter that are still prevalent in organic sheep farming.

Furthermore, the ban on antibiotics, vaccines, and other medications in organic production can be problematic and cause more misery for animals on organic facilities than on conventional operations.[23] If an animal is sick, the restrictions on pharmaceuticals to aid the animal can cause unnecessary suffering and a prolonging of illness, all for the profitable claim that organic products are untainted by medicine that desperately sick animals may be in need of.[24] Due to frequent forced pregnancy and milking, mastitis is common in dairy cows. Mastitis is a painful infection of the udder that causes tender, swollen teats and open sores.[25] Mastitis is usually treated with antibiotics; however, these medications are forbidden in organic dairies, and cows with mastitis must suffer numerous agonizing milkings every day with no relief. The label, and the higher prices that the label brings at the market, are more important to producers than reducing the suffering of the animals.

In the largest class-action lawsuit in organic agriculture, Aurora Organic Dairy was found guilty of willfully misleading consumers by keeping thousand of cows in atrocious factory-farming conditions with no access to pasture. The Cornucopia Institute, a farm policy research group and organic industry watchdog, blew the whistle on this major supplier of organic milk to Walmart, Costco, Target, and other retailers. Aurora was using marketing images and descriptions of cows happily grazing in a grassy pasture, when the reality was severe overcrowding on a filthy industrial-factory farm. They were also found guilty of bringing in cows that had been fed conventional feed and soon after selling the milk as organic, a blatant violation of organic regulations. The settlement was for $7.5 million to be paid out to misled customers. These kinds of false advertising lawsuits involving alternative animal product labeling are cropping up more and more as suppliers betray consumer trust and trick them into thinking animals are happy and healthy, when the reality is that they are no better than the industry standard.

Certified Humane and American Humane Certified

Humane Farm Animal Care, in conjunction with other animal welfare groups, offers the Certified Humane label. American Humane Certified is a similar certification, with about the same standards. These programs were created by animal-behavior scientists and veterinarians and are audited by physical inspection. These certifications do go beyond the usual standards of care. Dairy cows are required a minimum of four hours outdoors in pasture; gestation crates for pigs (single stalls for pregnant pigs where they are unable to turn around or lie down comfortably) and battery cages for hens are not allowed. Bedding is required for pigs and litter for hens, to dust bathe.

However, many of the horrors of animal farming are still allowed, even under the Certified Humane labels. Bodily mutilations are performed, like castration, tail-docking (cutting off the tail), and de-beaking, all without painkillers. There is no requirement for pigs or chickens to have access to the outside; babies are still taken away immediately upon or soon after birth; and beef cattle can languish in a muddy feedlot for months on end and still be labeled Certified Humane. And in the end, all these animals go to the same slaughterhouses as any other unfortunate animal being killed for his flesh.[26]

The wide variety of standards for labeling make it nearly impossible for the consumer to truly know what kind of care and treatment the animal received when it is neatly packaged with a feel-good label. With livestock production there is an inverse relationship between profit and compassion. Many cruelties in the industry are inherent, and producers could never make a profit if they changed their practices. In nature, these animals would live in family units; but in any animal agricultural, families are broken, the babies never know the love of a mother, and a mother endures the distress of the loss of her offspring. This will most certainly be the case in any farming operation, and always, for all of these condemned animals, the end result after suffering exploitation, violence, and hardship, will be death.

Most of these labels fail to regulate or consider standard industry practices that continue even on these supposedly humane farms. Painful procedures like debeaking, tail docking, dehorning, ear notching, castration, and teeth filing are the norm; there are no standards for safety and comfort in transport. The cruelty of the chick hatcheries, including the brutal killing of millions of baby male chicks is not addressed in any regulations pertaining to these labels.[27]

Lives Cut Short

Farm animals, whether born to a factory farm or an alternative operation, have their lives cut drastically short, and they are betrayed by their human caregivers, whose ultimate motive is to harvest their bodies for profit. Veal calves are slaughtered at only three to four months old; broiler chickens at around forty-two days, when they could live six years or more; pigs at six months, when they could live nine years or more; beef cattle at less than twenty-four months, when they could live twenty years or more; dairy cows at four to six years, when they could live twenty-five years or more. No matter what their lives are like, there is one thing that is certain—it will be short, and it will come to an unnatural end.[28]

For anyone who feels they must consume dairy, egg, or meat products, please deeply and honestly examine certain factors, such as whether you really *need* that product, whether the animal was treated as an individual with total respect and humanity, or whether you are simply preferring to believe what is most convenient rather than taking the time and effort to really know the reality behind the label. Reading this book is a great start, but many of these questions are very difficult to answer and you may never know as the general public cannot visit most of these farms. And even when you can visit, consumers are not shown the animal's entire life and experience, but offered a sterilized snapshot of the production reality. As this chapter has illustrated, it is impossible to produce meat, dairy, or eggs without inherent cruelty. Reducing and eventually abstaining from the use of animal products is the only truly humane option. Ethical eating can under no circumstances include the consumption of meat, dairy, and eggs from animals.

Chapter 4
Urban Eggs and Backyard Slaughter

When I look into the eyes of an animal, I do not see
an animal. I see a living being. I see a friend. I see
a soul.

—Anthony Douglas Williams,
Inside the Divine Pattern

There is a new trend, fueled by the local, slow, and sustainable food movements, of raising animals in urban backyards and "killing what you eat." This new fad is both encouraging and, at the same time, unsettling. Facebook tycoon Mark Zuckerburg challenged himself for a year to eat only the meat of animals he killed himself. Zuckerburg was obviously thinking about where his food comes from, and this is an advantageous first step on the road to compassionate eating. However, if one is genuinely concerned for the animal, why not take this line of reasoning to the healthy and logical conclusion and simply not eat animals? Zuckerburg admitted he was eating mostly vegetarian because of his vow and that it was troubling emotionally to kill a lobster,[1] as a lobster will claw the pot in a desperate attempt to flee the scalding water. Then why resort to killing at all?

It is a positive step that people are increasingly taking on this challenge to face the brutal reality of killing animals and many are finding that killing is a difficult and disturbing thing to do. The inclination to not turn a blind eye and pay someone else to "do the dirty work" is an opportunity to learn the truth about the suffering of animals killed for food. However, there is no moral conundrum with growing and harvesting tomatoes. With backyard slaughter, some people may be making an earnest attempt at practicing animal welfare, but ultimately the animal still suffers an untimely death—and a treacherous betrayal.

People who are concerned for animals should be aware of the new backyard hobby of raising and slaughtering animals. Urban farmers are approaching city-planning commissions and boards of supervisors across the country, proposing to change city ordinances to allow them to keep and kill livestock for profit. Goats, rabbits, chickens, and other fowl are finding themselves in small, urban backyards to be slaughtered, gutted, and headed for the dinner table or sold in local sales, with no regulation or oversight.

In California, the Oakland Food Policy Council recently submitted just such a proposal to the city planning commission, looking for clarification on its urban agriculture code. At first glance, this movement to allow growing and selling of vegetable crops in the city limits is a positive step toward getting healthy vegetables to "food desert" urban centers where vegetables and other healthy plant foods are scarce. However, the Oakland proposal also seeks to deregulate raising and slaughtering animals.[2]

There are numerous concerns with these proposals. Well-meaning, but inexperienced, hobbyists experimenting with raising their backyard herds and flocks will inevitably cause unintended misery. Animals require a great deal of experienced care, and vet bills are expensive. Many people find they can't afford health care for the animals, and they don't have time for proper cleaning and upkeep, so animals end up living in unsanitary conditions, leading to odors, pests, and disease, as well as discomfort and distress for the animals. Furthermore, most backyards are far too small for raising livestock, who need space to roam, graze, and express their essential natural behaviors.

Slaughtering animals in an urban setting is problematic as well. Botched slaughter jobs result in prolonged suffering during killing. Inexperience will lead to animals suffering extreme agony. Killing methods for rabbits are especially brutal, with names like "twist and crunch." The cry of a rabbit in distress is bone-chilling and not something that the neighborhood children should have to endure. Blood and animal parts not deemed edible are often illegally dumped in backyards, polluting local groundwater.

Jocelyn (photo credit: Animal Place)

Jocelyn, Madeline, and Andy

Jocelyn, Madeline, and Andy retreat when you approach them. Although they're timid and shy, it's worth the rejection to see their little bunny butts hop away. They exude cute even with their backs to you. These three rabbits living the good life in a shady outdoor area at Animal Place were formerly being raised in a backyard for their meat. Neighbors complained about the illegal operation, where they were not being cared for properly; they didn't have adequate shelter, water, or appropriate food. The bunnies were in bad shape when local authorities confiscated them. Marji Beach, of Animal Place said, "Rabbits are seen as companion animals by most people, and they are horrified when they learn that three million of them are slaughtered every year for food consumption." The method of slaughter used by this man was to put the rabbit's head on the ground and put a broomstick over the neck, hold the stick down with his feet and then yank the bunny's body up till the neck snapped. We dolefully reflected on how grateful we were that Jocelyn, Madeline, and Andy did not have to endure this frightening and cruel fate.

Underfunded city animal services simply do not have enough officers to investigate *existing* animal cruelty and neglect cases, much less the vastly amplified complaints that come from having increased livestock being raised and slaughtered in urban areas. There are already plenty of people who abuse and neglect animal companions; shelters are overwhelmed with dog and cats who have been starved, beaten, abandoned, and carelessly mistreated, with injuries and festering wounds. Imagine if animals that are socially acceptable to kill and eat were to be introduced to neighborhoods. Local animal services do not have the personnel to control and regulate every situation. If this trend continues to increase, many animals will be suffering right next door to unsuspecting neighbors.

Cruelty cases are not the only problematic issue of introducing farmed animals into a neighborhood. Public disturbances such as odor, noise, rat infestations, and escaped animals will be unwanted consequences as well. People who don't understand how labor intensive it is to care for livestock and how expensive it is, or who weren't prepared for the grizzly slaughtering process, will abandon and neglect these animals and further overwhelm agencies, shelters, and rescuers who can't handle the load of abandoned companion and farmed animals they already face.

Mocha (Photo Credit: Harvest Home)

Mocha and Coconut

The six recued goats at Harvest Home, a small farmed-animal sanctuary in Stockton, California, all came from urban properties. Christine Morrissey, the sanctuary's live-in volunteer, explains. "The reason they end up here is that people have no clue how to care for goats. They don't know the basics of nutrition or how they should be housed, and they end up being neglected or become sick or are in a situation where they shouldn't be. People think it's going to be easy, and it's simply not true. They end up causing more harm than should ever be necessary." Mocha and her sister, Coconut, were bought by a woman in Oakland to "mow" her land. She didn't provide any shelter or food and expected them to eat the weeds and brush, which will not yield enough nutrition for goats to remain healthy. Neighbors became increasingly concerned about the skinny, sickly goats, who were left out in the elements. They convinced the negligent guardian to relinquish Mocha and Coconut to Harvest Home.

> Christine said there is a similar narrative for the other goats at the sanctuary. "It's like the same story on repeat for the other goats; people say they want to use them as lawnmowers. People think they can eat everything, they can eat tin cans. It just demonstrates how little information people have about them."

People who participate in do-it-yourself slaughter have a false sense of entitlement to meat eating because they have "participated in the process." Facing the horror of slaughter firsthand offers them an artificial and romanticized connection to meat eating. Therefore, they often do not feel that they need to limit their meat eating to alternative sources, and they become more avid meat eaters.[3]

Growing plant-based foods provides more food per acre than even local organic animal agriculture can. With the environmental and climate crisis looming, we must maximize the agricultural output of every acre of land. In California, the Oakland Food Policy Council (OFPC) created the Oakland Food System Assessment, which calculated how much usable land would be needed to feed 30 percent of Oakland residents with locally grown food. They found that they would need nine thousand acres to feed 30 percent of the community using vegetable farming. If animal foods were included, it would require ten thousand *additional* acres, totaling nineteen thousand acres to feed the same number of people.[4] That is land that most cities do not have to spare. The planet cannot afford for us to eat high on the food chain anymore.

Most people starting a backyard flock get their chicks by mail order from hatcheries. As explained in previous chapters, hatcheries are huge, sterile facilities were the chicks are hatched in metal drawers and peck their way into the world not to a mother and warm nest, but to the cold, harsh reality of machines, conveyer belts, and the indifferent hand of a worker roughly tossing them about. They are shipped via the US Postal Service in dark cardboard boxes with no temperature control, food, or water sometimes for days. They are bashed about like canned goods and loud noises from trucks and airplanes create panic and fear among the newborns.[5] Ten percent arrive dead at their destination. The hatcheries always pack more chicks than the order called for due to this unfortunate reality. The dead chicks are considered packing material and are called "packers." So, despite the attempts of urban backyard hobby enthusiasts to defy industrial agriculture, they are often still supporting some of the worst practices in the industry by purchasing chicks from hatcheries.

Reggie (photo credit: Farm Sanctuary)

Reggie

In Sonoma County, California, a journalist with a prominent newspaper in the area, decided to raise a pig, slaughter him at a local event, and write about the experience, in an effort to explore the mounting questions of knowing where our food comes from. She bought Reggie Bacon for $180 from a local rancher. Reggie had delightful black-and-white bicoloring which, interestingly, is only found in domesticated animals. It is not a beneficial camouflage but bred by humans to identify individuals in groups and also because we find it endearing. Reggie Bacon needed to put on a few more pounds before his death sentence could be carried out, and the journalist penned an article about her endeavor in the paper. Local animal advocates were horrified to learn of Reggie's plight and contacted the journalist, respectfully pleading for Reggie's life. The journalist, becoming more and more fond of Reggie as a charming individual, agreed to meet with the animal people to discuss the matter. Eventually her conscience wouldn't let her go through with her experiment. She agreed to turn Reggie over to the activists, and they found him a home with Farm Sanctuary in Orland, California, a rare happy ending for a member of his condemned species.

Let's take a look at some individual cases of "compassionate carnivores" and their own blogged accounts of backyard animal farming.

This one, regarding killing a chicken, is from *Poor Girl Gourmet*,[6] in Rehoboth, Massachusetts.

> We researched humane slaughter practices, including chicken hypnosis; however, the practice round of hypnosis failed miserably, and we came to believe that piercing the chicken's brain would be the least traumatic for all involved. Not so. On that fateful day, JR [her husband] placed the chicken into the cone, where it promptly

attempted to somersault its way out of the guillotine, clawing furiously at the sloping plastic walls, pushing its head up as though it might get to see the sun again. JR took a pair of sharp scissors—this is a judgment call we lived to regret; despite having an ice pick given to us for this very purpose, we went with the alternative, sharp-scissor implement. As it turns out, the chicken brain is a very small target, and one that is easily missed. I went from enthusiastic documentary photographer to gagging wife in the span of approximately a half a second. With camera now useless and my retching instinct fully intact, JR grabbed his sharpened hedge trimmers. Oh, if only they were truly sharp, those sharpened hedge trimmers. The trimmers did not succeed in lopping off the head of the poor, tortured chicken. Instead, they folded its neck over itself in a zigzag crease, which did, at least, succeed in breaking its neck, and therefore killing it.

And this one is from the blog *High Desert Chronicles.*[7]

And I won't lie, it wasn't easy. I was shaking so badly on the first one I was afraid I'd cut myself with the knife I was using to skin them. It's a little gruesome if you think too hard about it— there are details I wasn't emotionally prepared for, which I'm about to talk about, so if you're reading this comment and feeling squeamish, you may want to skip to the next one … Some of the difficult details: the way it moves around after the head is gone, and the times when the head doesn't come off cleanly, and the time when I picked one up to skin it and it started jumping around again after I stuck the knife in it (it was headless).

Another from Novella Carpenter, of Ghost Town Farm in the city of Oakland, California.

I feel like I'm orchestrating a murder. It's very complicated. So many details. Like, who's going to kill them? How will I transport the pigs to the assassin? Does my friend's truck have a trailer hitch with a functioning light? Etc. In short, I'm freaking out. A friend of mine asked if I'm going to miss the pigs, and I didn't hesitate: absolutely not. They're so much work to feed. They're ill-mannered/rude. They fight over food. They attract flies. And finally, no spider has spun a web with pro-pig slogans. So I'm going forward. (September 5, 2007)

"Want to see a baby goat?" I brought him into her room. "Don't get attached," I said. "He's not going to make it."

"Can't you save him?" Trista asked.

"Probably not, plus he's a boy—worthless in the dairy business." (September 4, 2011)

It continues with excerpts from the blog of Esperanza Pallana, of Pluck and Feather Farm, also in Oakland.

I am often asked if I break the necks of my poultry, and I do not. I thought, since I had someone right there with me, I would personally attempt this by hand with my rabbit ... mistake. I was not strong, and sure enough, maybe my arms are not long enough. Whatever it is, I shall not attempt that again if I can help it. (September 15, 2009)

And another from the blog *Original Country Girl*[8] in Northern Wisconsin.

The best advice is to always maintain a distance between you and those intended for your dinner plate. This makes the butchering much easier if the animal is nothing more than "the black chicken" or "the grey-and-white goose." You can care for your critters in a humane and respectful way without allowing attachments to form. Rule number one is to never give it a name. Some people can get by with ironic names like the aforementioned "Christmas dinner" moniker, but for others even this can cause trouble later on. If you know you're soft-hearted, *don't do it!* Clean the pen, feed good feed, and tend any wounds, but don't get too close. No names, no handfed treats, and no special treatment for any one individual animal.

Apart from the obvious violence here, it is important to note the degree of betrayal. These are animals who live within close proximity to their human guardians. Backyard hobbyists express the need to care for the animals and "clean the pen, feed good feed, and tend any wounds." But even if the level of care is more humane than an animal would receive in an industrial counterpart, this does not necessarily mean that the backyard slaughter enthusiast is on any sort of moral high ground. As we have argued in the first chapter, any increased ethical consideration given to the better treatment of the animal is nullified by the greater transgression of betrayal. The animals may live better and therefore come to trust the human captor more. With this increased expectation there is an increased obligation—and a greater sense of betrayal. Where there is better care there is greater trust. And where there is greater trust there is greater betrayal. Therefore, it follows that these animals are suffering an extreme form of betrayal, one that can only come with proximity and perceived protection. While we can be betrayed by our friends and enemies alike, the betrayal that we suffer by those who are close to us is the more malicious and hurtful kind. That is the betrayal suffered by animals who are victims of the backyard slaughter hobbyist.

This is not to say that it is more ethical to torture an animal and then kill it because the factor of betrayal would be less if the animal was abused. Obviously, torturing and abusing animals is in itself a severe ethical transgression. What we are saying here is that when the abuse is less, it is proportionally replaced with the infraction of betrayal, that is to say: the lesser the abuse, the greater the bond of trust that forms, and therefore the greater the act of betrayal. So the animal is either being betrayed or abused or both. When an animal is killed for the interests of the human captor, as they are in these backyard operations, the treatment of the animal while it is alive will inevitably be unethical, whether that source of cruelty comes from betrayal or abuse.

Animals should not be included in the future of local urban farming. We need to act compassionately, be an example for our children, and be forward-thinking beyond backyard slaughter. The desire to know where you food comes from and to be part of the process is an admirable aspiration. Plant a garden. There is never a moral question about picking the pole beans. There is no fear of getting too close to your carrots. There is no horrible trepidation around the method of harvesting honeydew. No blood and guts, just dirt and weeds.

Animals are companions to be enjoyed, friends to share our lives, allies in the enjoyment of experiencing existence. Feel empathy; please, get too close to them. We need more compassion in our lives, not more violence and killing. Farmed animals have no place in an urban setting unless they are companion animals, respected and loved in the same way as our dogs and cats. If a chicken is a loved companion, cared for and sheltered, with plenty of space and protection at night; if she is given veterinary care and is able to live out her full natural lifespan; and if the guardian uses the eggs and shares the eggs for no monetary gain, this can be an ethical situation. However, the health impact of the cholesterol-laden egg should be considered. We will investigate the health implications of animal products in chapter 10.

Let's expand our circle of compassion to include all animals under the same consideration as our dog, who we would never consider slaughtering for dinner. Chickens, rabbits, and all other animals share the same capacity for love as our adored dog or cat. Let's not betray the trust that an animal whom we are caring for has bestowed upon us by one day turning on him and viciously killing him. It is completely unnecessary in our first-world smorgasbord of plant-food options. Enjoy a cruelty-free diet; there is no need to get blood on your hands.

ALAMEDA FREE LIBRARY

Part 2
The Ultimate Betrayal of the Earth

Chapter 5
Eco-Eating: A Cool Diet
for a Hot Planet

*Environmentalists who ignore the ecological cost of
producing meat are in denial of one of the greatest
threats to the world's ecosystems and the prospect of
eating ethically.*

—James McWilliams, *Just Food*

With all the dire environmental predictions, we could use some
good news. Well, there is some *great* news for the planet. The
food and drink an average person consumes is the single largest
determining factor of one's overall ecological footprint.[1] Why
is this good news? Because once we become aware of this, it is
easy and affordable to make important improvements to our
global impact. We don't need to buy hybrid cars or get solar
panels to make the biggest difference, although these changes
can also be extremely beneficial. Just changing our shopping and
eating habits to delicious plant-based choices can have profoundly
positive effects. No lavish expenses on green technology or severe
austerities are required. Our food choices in themselves have the

most dramatic consequences on the health of our environment. Reducing or eliminating the consumption of animal products is one of the most powerful ways we can reduce our carbon footprint. What we put into our bags at the grocery store can actually have more environmental impact than whether we bring reusable shopping bags or drive eco-vehicles to the store.

Environmental Ethics

Metaphorically speaking, we can think of our lives as being a contract with the Earth. The planet provides us with all that we need to live healthy and productive lives, and we, in turn, are morally obligated to ensure that we live in such a way that future generations of humans, plants, and animals will be afforded the same opportunity to thrive that we were. We have a responsibility to the edicts of justice that we are bound to by simply being alive.

To illustrate, imagine if someone close to you were to win the lottery and decided that because you were such a dear person to them that you should partake in their fortune, and they bestowed several millions of dollars upon you. Would you not feel a great deal of gratitude, obligation, and indebtedness toward your benefactor? Even if this person did not expect anything in return, you would still be morally obligated to not take this grand gift for granted, and you would feel highly compelled to be of whatever service you could to this beneficent person. This is even more emphatic with respect to reciprocity with our planet. It is because of our earth's bounty and charity that we are able to sustain our lives. The gift of life is much greater than any monetary value that could be placed upon it. The life that we enjoy in the form of fresh air, healthy soil, clean water, and abundant sustenance is perhaps the greatest gift that we could ever receive.

Going back to the analogy, imagine that your benefactor falls ill with a debilitating and life-threatening disease, and you are a doctor capable of helping him. But you don't, because you are enjoying the luxury you received from your now-dying friend. This scenario would be unthinkable, as we put such a high value on human life, but what about the life of our home—our planet—the Earth? Whether or not you choose to attribute the life-giving abundance of the Earth to a divine magnanimity, we can all agree that this gift of life comes to us through the medium of our planetary ecology. Therefore, we all owe a great debt to our precious blue planet, the only one we know of that supports life as we know it. We have caused her illness and we have the power to heal her.

The Earth gives us life. We need her air to breathe, her water to drink, and her temperate climate to survive. She offers her wealth of resources freely for the taking; it is our ethical duty to not take more than we need and to not destroy the rest. To do so is to extinguish ourselves. To waste her resources, to pollute her water, or to alter her climate, is a betrayal of a sacred life-supporting contract and ultimately a betrayal of ourselves. We betray our future by damaging our only home. People with children should be especially attuned to this; we betray our responsibility to our children by condemning them to a future in the shattered environment we discard in our wake.

Morality dictates more from us than an obligation to our great Earth. We also have a responsibility to the higher virtue of justice in our relationship with other living beings. If we enjoy opulence and excesses at the expense of others, then we have transgressed the boundaries of fairness. Therefore, to be ethical people, we must live in a way that allows other species and future generations to have the same opportunity that we have received ourselves. If we take more than we need to survive, it is at the expense of others. This is why it is wrong to kill animals for simple gluttony.

The same can be said for our consumption of natural resources. If we consume resources in such a way that we are simply indulging in unnecessary extravagances, or for convenience, at the expense of the needs of others (human and nonhuman), then we are committing injustice. Perhaps the most egregious example of our excessive consumption comes in the form of our dietary rapacity. The environmental consequences of these choices constitute a betrayal toward those who depend on us to equitably share the resources of the planet, both human and nonhuman.

We are not arguing that it is wrong to enjoy what a modern life offers; nor advocating for any sort of extreme self-denial of material accouterments. However, humanity needs to live up to the altruistic connotations of our own self-appointed appellation by examining the ramifications of our patterns of consumption and choices. Think before taking action: How much do I gain from this, and how much does it cost others and the Earth? Often just a small shift in choice can offer great benefit: ecologically friendly laundry and dish soap; recycled paper products; weeding instead of using Roundup; buying used items instead of new; plant-based milk replacing dairy; vegetables, rice, and beans in the place of meat.

If someone eats animal products, it is highly unlikely that they obtain them exclusively from alternative sources, as these products make up only about 1 percent of the market. If they eat out, unless they are lucky enough to live in a few select major cities where there may be a couple of restaurants offering organic meats, consumers are likely getting at least some, if not the majority, of their animal products from conventional sources. Whether meat, dairy, and eggs come from industrial agribusiness or an alternative farm, just using the resources to keep billions of farmed animals alive causes enormous environmental impact. The following explores the bigger picture of that impact. In chapter 6 we will have a closer look at alternative animal farming and its effect on our planet.

Our Changing Climate

What do the Pentagon, the United Nations, The Union of Concerned Scientists, and Greenpeace all have in common? Wait, the Pentagon and Greenpeace have something in common? They do! They all believe that global warming is real and that animal agriculture significantly contributes to climate change.[2, 3, 4, 5]

Animal agriculture is responsible for many of the world's most serious environmental problems—global warming, water use and pollution, massive energy consumption, deforestation, loss of biodiversity and species, as well as the deep impact that fishing has on our oceans.[6] A 2010 Report from the United Nations International Panel for Sustainable Resource Management *strongly urges a global shift to a plant-based diet* to both feed a hungry world and greatly reduce environmental impacts like global warming. Professor Edgar Hertwich, the lead author of the report said that "animal products cause more damage than [producing] construction minerals such as sand or cement, plastics or metals. Biomass and crops for animals are as damaging as [burning] fossil fuels."[7]

Our planet is rapidly changing. Killer tornados and superstorms, massive floods, and devastating droughts are becoming common occurrences worldwide. Bizarre and unpredictable weather is the new normal. The Intergovernmental Panel on Climate Change (IPCC), consisting of a Nobel Prize–winning panel of climate scientists, released a report in the spring of 2012 with dire predictions: extreme weather patterns will rapidly increase and have distressing effects on highly populated coastal regions—from Miami to Mumbai. Increasingly intense tropical storms, heat waves, droughts, and deluges will adversely affect some of the world's poorest and most vulnerable populations.[8]

The freakishly dramatic weather events of the first decade of the 2000s were documented in a 2011 study of the World Meteorological Association called *Weather Extremes in a Changing Climate*. Here are just some of the highlights. In 2001, Alaska had the warmest winter on record, and Canada recorded another warmer-than-average season—the eighteenth in a row. The year 2003 saw record heat waves, including Europe's hottest summer since 1540. The sweltering heat caused up to seventy thousand deaths across Europe. In 2004, ten cyclones made a record in Japan, and in 2005, the world faced twenty-seven named tropical storms that included fourteen hurricanes, an extraordinary number of weather eruptions. And it just keeps getting worse.

In 2005, the most active hurricane season ever recorded, Hurricane Katrina hit the United States' Gulf Coast hard and killed over thirteen hundred people. The year 2006 saw the worst flooding in Africa in fifty years; meanwhile, the United States was parched and saw a most devastating wildfire season as a result. On the other side of the world, a typhoon hit Southeast Asia and killed twelve hundred people in the Philippines. In 2007, Alaska saw its second-longest frost-free season on record, and Mexico experienced devastating floods that caused the worst weather-related disaster in its history. In 2008, the heavy snow and freezing temperatures of the most brutal winter in fifty years affected seventy-eight million people in China; one and a half million people were affected by flooding in Brazil; and Myanmar saw its worst natural disaster ever, when Cyclone Nargis hit with maximum winds of 134 mph. In 2009, 170 people died in brushfires caused by unprecedented heat waves in Australia, and to top off the decade, 2010 ranked the warmest year on record. [9] Global warming is not something off in the future that will effect generations to come; it is here—now. Each year, every day, more greenhouse gasses are released. We must take fast and decisive action in order to stop careening toward increasingly cataclysmic weather events that effect everyone, humans and wildlife alike.

When it comes to climate change, farmed animals and their by-products are responsible for 51 percent of annual worldwide human-caused greenhouse gas emissions. This is according to a report published in *World Watch Magazine* written by prominent World Bank Group environmental specialists, Jeff Anhang and Robert Goodland. Based on their research, they conclude that replacing animal products with plant-based foods worldwide would be the best strategy for reversing climate change. They advise that this can reduce emissions even more than the current trajectory to replace fossil fuels with renewable energy.[10] The current proposal of transitioning to renewable energy is a slow, costly, and initially energy-intensive process, and we are running out of time. A global shift to a plant-based diet would require comparatively minimal infrastructure change and could take effect much more quickly, creating emissions reductions immediately.

The United Nations Food and Agriculture Committee also looked at animal agriculture's impact on the environment in a study called *Livestock's Long Shadow*. In this groundbreaking document, they cite climate change, freshwater scarcity, and depleting biodiversity and species as significant harms caused by livestock rearing worldwide. The report states, "livestock's contribution to environmental problems is on a massive scale ... The impact is so significant, it needs to be addressed with urgency."[11] It continues, "the livestock sector has such deep and wide-ranging environmental impacts that it should rank as one of the leading focuses of environmental policy."[12]

Furthermore, a study by the University of Chicago found that abstaining from the consumption of animal products is *50 percent more effective* at fighting global warming than switching from a standard car to a hybrid.[13] This is because several gasses contribute to the greenhouse effect, not only the notorious carbon dioxide (CO_2) that results from burning fossil fuels. Others are methane, with 72 times the global warming potential than carbon dioxide and nitrous oxide, with 310 times the heat-trapping power of carbon dioxide. A single pound of methane has the same greenhouse effect as approximately 50 pounds of carbon dioxide. Of all human activities that cause these gasses, 65 percent of nitrous oxide and almost 40 percent of methane comes from livestock production.[14]

Another significant difference in these gasses is how long it takes for them to leave the atmosphere. Carbon dioxide stays in the atmosphere for hundreds of years. While reducing CO_2 is important, when the reduction of our emissions of CO_2 finally occurs, we will not see a corresponding reduction in temperature for generations to come. Methane and nitrous oxide, on the other hand, disperse in the atmosphere much more quickly, with methane dissipating almost entirely in eight to twelve years after emission. Therefore, a reduction of methane and nitrous oxide will go further toward our more immediate chances of temperature reduction worldwide. In the study *Livestock and Climate Change*, coauthors Goodland and Anhang state, "Although methane warms the atmosphere much more strongly than does CO_2, its half-life in the atmosphere is only about eight years, versus at least one hundred years for CO_2. As a result, a significant reduction in livestock raised worldwide would reduce GHGs relatively quickly compared with measures involving renewable energy and energy efficiency [measures that mostly target CO2 emissions]."

A 2012 report from the World Preservation Foundation recommends reduction of these greenhouse gasses, saying, "Commercially viable solutions to reduce these shorter-lived causes of climate change exist today, with a dietary change away from animal proteins, toward plant proteins, being the most attractive for its ability to reduce emissions quickly and inexpensively." The report went on to tout the switch from animal to plant foods with this, "as well as for the additional benefits of contributing significantly to reversing biodiversity loss, ensuring water and food security, substantially reducing tropical deforestation, and reducing healthcare costs."[15]

They also found that a global switch to a plant-based diet would create an 87 percent dietary reduction of greenhouse-gas emissions with conventional [nonorganic] plant foods and a 94 percent reduction with organic plant foods. That is compared to a measly 8 percent reduction by switching from conventional meat and dairy to "sustainable" animal products.[16]

Unfortunately, recognizing animal products for the global-warming culprits they are involves significant abstract thinking. Identifying carbon emissions from, let's say, a car is much more observable. The fossil fuel is pumped into the car in the form of gas and emits its by-products from the tail pipe. How much fuel we burn by driving our cars is calculated by the fuel gauge, and through this we are directly aware of the impact on the environment inflicted by our transportation habits on a daily basis. But an animal product sits deceivingly innocent in a plastic-wrapped package, with no clear way to tally its heavy environmental toll, so the greatest source of destruction to the environment is largely hidden from our direct experience.

How does an animal product come to have such a profound carbon footprint? There is a combination of factors. Producing animal products wastes enormous amounts of energy and fossil fuels, emitting vast quantities of greenhouse gasses in the process. Throw in the destruction of the Amazon rainforest for cattle grazing and raising grains fed to animals, and you have a recipe for significant contribution to climate change.

There are direct and indirect emission factors attributed to the entire process of getting a living, breathing four-legged or feathered creature to become an unrecognizable, dismembered piece of meat on a plate. Direct impact comes from the now-infamous bodily functions of cows emitting methane into the atmosphere. Although flatulence seems to get the majority of snickers, it is predominantly cow burps that release the most methane. Along with the cow's digestive process, other direct impacts include deforestation to raise feed and graze cattle and dissemination of methane and nitrous oxide from decomposing mountains of manure and wet-waste lagoons. Indirect emissions come from the burning of fossil fuel to make fertilizer for cattle feed, the highly mechanized slaughter and processing plants draining considerable energy, and soil erosion from overgrazing. Another factor not often considered, albeit more minor, is that meat is frequently cooked at higher temperatures and for longer periods of time than vegetables and grains, causing home and restaurant stoves to consume more energy.

Plant-Based Meats Are Greener

A study out of Vienna by the Sustainable European Research Institute, commissioned by the German Vegetarian Society and the Austrian branch of the international environmental activist network Greenpeace, compared soy meat (tofu, and other soy-based products, as well as *seitan*, a wheat meat) to ground cow meat for their ecological impact. Researchers found that one kilogram of ground cow meat created 7,200 grams of carbon dioxide as compared with the same amount of soy food releasing only 350 grams of CO_2. That translates to about 90 percent fewer greenhouse gas emissions from the plant-based proteins.

The study also found that it takes 98 percent less land to produce the soy foods as compared to the meat. The study considered factors like water consumption, transportation, and the use of renewable and nonrenewable resources.[17] They calculated that if Germans replaced their annual per capita consumption of twelve kilograms of ground meat with meat alternatives, the CO_2 savings would be equal to taking four to seven million automobiles off the road.

Energy Consumption

A massive amount of energy is wasted in the artificial environments of the factory farm, slaughterhouse, and processing plant. These indoor environments have conveyer belts, milking machines, lighting, heating, and a highly mechanized slaughter process. Just in the transportation of the animals there are numerous steps. For instance, first the grain and other feed additives are transported to the animals, then the animals are transported to auction, then those animals are transported to slaughterhouses, then the carcasses are often processed and packaged in another facility, and finally, the product is transported one last time to the supermarket or restaurant. Compare that to a vegetable farmer who drives directly from his farm to the farmers' market or takes his vegetables from the farm to processing and then to the grocery store.

It takes eight times as much fossil fuel to produce animal food as it takes to produce plant food. Even the *least* efficient plant food is nearly ten times as efficient as the *most* energy-efficient animal food.[18] So what does that mean? Someone may be strolling the grocery aisles and think that a carton of milk from a local organic dairy must have less of a carbon footprint then a mango from Central America. Just think how far that mango must have traveled to reach our little health-food store. How many borders did it have to cross to land in the United States? It *must* have a heavier environmental toll than that local animal product. This way of thinking only takes into account food miles, but the bigger picture is how much energy was wasted in production, and animal products are incredibly energy intensive in production, often having a much heavier footprint than any plant foods. We will delve much deeper into the "local" fallacy in the next chapter.

Stated more succinctly:

Meat-centered diet = SUV

Vegetarian diet = mid-sized car

Vegan diet = biking or walking[19]

The Air We Must Breathe

Beyond releasing greenhouse gasses, the practice of farming animals also releases a host of pollutants into the air, including hydrogen sulfate, ammonia, and other particulate matter. Airborne particulates can irritate respiratory systems and cause asthma, decrease lung function, and when lodged in lung tissue, increase risk for heart attacks and death. Ammonia and hydrogen sulfide can cause eye and lung irritations, neurological symptoms, and with long-term or high concentration exposure, premature death.

The animal-agriculture industry releases toxins into the air on an industrial scale, yet the industry has managed to avoid regulations put in place to protect communities surrounding them. In 2005, the Environmental Protection Agency (EPA) offered the animal agriculture industry a deal that stunk almost as much as the mountains of excrement on the farms. They would be exempt from any regulations while an excruciatingly long-term study of harmful emissions was conducted. In 2008, they were still, shamefully, excluded from most air-quality regulation.[20]

Federal law requires most industries to report ammonia output if it is greater than one hundred pounds per day, yet animal agriculture is exempt. A study by the Environmental Integrity Project reported that eleven of fourteen farms tested released more than one hundred pounds of ammonia in a typical day, and some released into the thousands of pounds. The biggest offenders were hog farms, dairy facilities, egg producers, and broiler (chickens raised for meat) operations. There were similar findings cited for excessive levels of hydrogen sulfate in hog and dairy operations. The scientists conclude, "This study adds to a growing body of research showing that factory farms are industrial-scale polluters, and EPA's failure to regulate CAFO (Concentrated Animal Feeding Operations) pollution under the Clean Air Act and other laws runs afoul of sound science."[21]

The Water We Must Drink

For the sake of our animal-centered menus, a vital and precious natural resource is being drained to dangerously low levels— clean, fresh water. Most of the world's water is used for irrigation of crops, and most of that agricultural irrigation is connected to animals. Agricultural production, including livestock production, consumes more fresh water than any other activity in the United States; in fact, agricultural irrigation accounts for 85 percent of the fresh water consumed.[22] Not only does it take vast amounts of water to hydrate the animals, over half the total amount of fresh water consumed in the United States goes to irrigate land to grow feed for livestock. Additionally, huge amounts of water are used to clean the blood and grease from the equipment in the butchering process, to wash excrement down the drain, etc. A dairy operation that utilizes an automatic flushing system can use up to 150 gallons of water per cow, per day.[23]

The Ogallala Aquifer is located beneath the Great Plains in the United States. This vast, yet shallow, underground water table is one of the world's largest aquifers, covering an area of approximately 174,000 square miles; it spans beneath eight states. The Ogallala provides drinking water to 82 percent of the people living above it and in the surrounding areas, but this finite water source is being drained dry to water animals. The states above the Ogallala are some of the most productive regions for ranching livestock and for growing the corn and soybeans to feed them. This region does not have adequate precipitation and doesn't always have perennial surface water for diversion. Its success has depended heavily on pumping groundwater from the Ogallala for irrigation.

Ninety percent of the water drained from the Ogallala is used for agricultural irrigation, the vast majority of which is connected to animal agriculture. The reservoir is so low that it has already dried up in some areas. If it were to be drained completely, scientists say that it would take six thousand years for nature to replenish it.[24] The Great Plains will see its own devastating dust bowl if water levels continue to drop.

At the Stockholm International Water Institute, leading scientists specialized in the study of the world's water supply issued a dire warning—with the population expected to reach nine billion by 2050, there will not be enough water to irrigate the food to feed everyone on the planet with our current dietary choices. What was their proposed solution? Switching to an almost completely vegetarian diet would solve the problem. The researchers said, "there will be just enough water if the proportion of animal-based foods is limited to five percent of total calories." They warn of catastrophic water and food shortages if action is not taken swiftly and meat consumption is not reduced worldwide.[25]

A cow can drink up to twenty-three gallons of water a day; humans, in comparison, drink less than one gallon.[26] That is a huge amount of water just to keep these animals alive. It takes less water to produce one year's worth of food for a completely plant-based diet than it does to produce one month's worth of food for a diet with animal products. Producing one pound of animal protein requires about *one hundred times more water* than producing one pound of grain protein.[27] Another study adds to the flood of evidence by stating that the amount of water needed to produce one pound of beef is almost 1,600 gallons, compared to just 102 gallons for a pound of wheat.[28] It has even been said that a vegan can leave the shower running for a year and still not waste as much water as a meat eater in the same year.

The crops we have chosen to quickly fatten up our farm animals are wasting water as well. Corn and soybeans represent the vast majority of livestock's diet. These two crops are incredibly cheap as a result of government subsidies, but these crops are also *exogenous*; they have a deeper thirst for water than *endogenous* crops, which are dormant in the warm summer months when there is a high demand for water. Exogenous crops require more water and are therefore yet another drain on an already wasteful system of processing animal products.[29]

Water Pollution

The millions of tons of waste produced by these massive farm-animal populations accumulate on the land and pollute our lakes, rivers, and groundwater. Water pollution and ammonia emissions, mainly from livestock production, compromise biodiversity—often drastically, in the case of aquatic life. Animal feed lots create more water pollution than factories and sewage-treatment plants.[30]

When animals are free roaming, their excrement is spread out over vast territories, naturally fertilizing the earth. However, when you have a mass of animals confined to a dairy operation or egg-laying facility, massive mountains of feces concentrate and leach into the groundwater, carrying antibiotics and hormones, blood and fluids from birthing, rodent poisons, cleaning solvents, and other contaminants into our waterways.

The livestock of the United States produce twenty times more excrement then the entire human population of the country.[31] One dairy farm with 2,500 cows produces as much solid waste as a city with about 411,000 residents.[32] Miami, Florida, with a population of 409,000 people, creates less waste than this dairy farm. With little or no requirements for sewage and water treatment for animal agriculture, the result is an ecological toll equivalent to a bustling city with every farmed-animal operation.

Some dairy, hog, and other animal facilities will attempt to contain the problem with what are called waste lagoons. These massive pools of liquid poop can cover up to eighteen acres and can be as deep as twenty-five feet.[33] As the liquid waste decomposes, the manure emits harmful gasses, such as nitrous oxide, methane, hydrogen sulfide, and ammonia, which is one of the leading causal factors of acid rain.[34] This toxic soup is far from contained as heavy rain causes overflow and groundwater leaching is common.[35] There is considerable contamination with waste lagoons, as rain and runoff leach viruses, bacteria, antibiotics, growth hormones, nitrates, and heavy metals, contaminating local water supplies.[36] You certainly don't want to live anywhere near one of these cesspools, as not only is the groundwater being contaminated, but the stench can invade the nostrils for miles.

Dead Zones

In North America, 48 percent of lakes are *eutrophic*, meaning that they are contaminated by excess nutrients like phosphorus and nitrogen from manure.[37] This nutrient overload in the water causes an extreme burst of plant growth; algae and other aquatic weeds thrive. They deplete the oxygen levels, block light to other plants, and asphyxiate bottom dwellers such as crabs and oysters. Unsuspecting fish swim into this oxygen-deprived area, lose consciousness, and die. These oxygen-depleted waters are referred to as dead zones.

The second-largest zone of coastal hypoxia (oxygen-depleted waters) in the world is found on the northern Gulf of Mexico, adjacent to the outflows of the Mississippi, where massive amounts of agricultural waste, manure, and pesticides flow down the now-polluted river to the Gulf. This twenty-thousand-square-kilometer dead zone is not alone.[38] Dead zones are appearing all over the world; they are so named because nothing can live in these waters where the oxygen has been exhausted.

Deforestation

Forests help purify the air and reduce carbon dioxide; they are home to many species of animals, birds, insects, and plants. Animal agriculture destroys thousands of acres of forests each year, and scientists are now estimating that half the world's rainforest could be completely destroyed by 2030. Cattle ranching is now the primary reason for deforestation in the Amazon."[39]

If you think of our planet as a living, breathing organism, the forests are the lungs. They create a perfect balance to our own respiratory process by absorbing millions of tons of CO_2 into the soil and exhaling oxygen into the air, exactly what is needed to maintain equilibrium of animal life with plant life and create the livable atmosphere we all enjoy. However, we are losing this integral part of our ecosystem on a massive scale, and it is largely due to the persistence of meat centered diets. Seventy percent of our planet's rainforests have already been slashed and burned in order to raise livestock and to grow the soybeans and other crops used to feed them. This irreversible loss continues by the minute.[40] When we lose an acre of rainforest, we not only lose its CO_2 sequestering power and oxygen production, we also lose the estimated five million species of plant, animal, and insect life that call the rainforest home, some of which are as yet undiscovered. Dozens of species each day are estimated to be disappearing, and scientists are calculating that we are losing plant and animal life now at one thousand to ten thousand times the natural rate.[41] Undiscovered and unnamed species and possible cures for deadly diseases disappear with every acre destroyed.

The result of deforestation is often the desertification of that area, with the soil degraded beyond the ability to support plant life. Latin America is facing mass desertification, with 70 percent of pastures mismanaged and trampled. A vast, dry desert is replacing the lush vegetation of the Americas as animal grazing continues.

Large-scale dietary change to a plant-based diet could actually reverse deforestation. In the United States, over four hundred million acres of pastureland, currently home to cows, could be reforested.[42] That is not to mention the hundreds of millions of additional acres that are used to grow feed for pigs, chickens, turkeys, and other farmed animals, most of which could be reforested. It is estimated that one acre of trees is preserved each year by each individual who switches to a completely plant-based diet.

Wildlands and Wildlife

Almost every large mammal in the United States is threatened or endangered, except for humans and the animals that people eat. In many cases, it is livestock rearing that has caused the wild animals to disappear. When animals are on the range, predation is a cause of lost revenue for livestock enterprises, so wildlife in the surrounding area is shot, poisoned, gassed, snared, or caught in steel-jaw leghold traps. Traps and snares are indiscriminate and kill non-target species like birds, badgers, squirrels, and various others. Even if the target predator is caught in the trap, he could painfully languish, starving for days, before finally being found and killed. A mother could be helplessly trapped and her cubs slowly starve to death back in the den, tragically killing the entire family.

Wildlife Services (formerly called Animal Damage Control) is a program of the United States Department of Agriculture whose sole purpose is to suppress and eradicate any wildlife considered damaging to US ranchers. Every year they spend millions of dollars to kill millions of animals as a "service" to our livestock industry.

Predators like coyotes, wolves, bears, mountain lions, and many others are indiscriminately killed just for being in the surrounding area of livestock. No predation of the domestic animals needs to have occurred. Methods of "removal" are poisons, gasses, leghold traps, and neck snares. Some animals are chased with hounds or helicopters, and after a terrifying and exhausting pursuit, they are either ripped up by the dogs or shot to death. Wildlife Services killed over five million animals in 2010.[43] If we were to remove the livestock, wildlife would again be allowed to flourish.

One shoddy argument for ranging animals is that the land that is used for livestock is unsuitable for growing plant foods. This line of reasoning misses the fact that there are already acres and acres of land growing tons of grain and other crops to feed farmed animals. This food could be diverted directly to humans, and the land that the animals are grazing on could be reclaimed by nature for wildlife, plant life, and trees, aiding carbon sequestering and helping curb global warming. And let's ponder for a moment *why* that land is unfit to grow anything—perhaps it's because it has been trampled again and again by very large mammals confined in the area by fences for many years? Grazing livestock takes a profound toll on the earth. The soil becomes compacted; heavy hooves cause erosion, runoff, desertification, and the loss of plant, animal, and insect life surrounding the area.

Wasting Resources and World Hunger

Year after year we waste millions of all-you-can-eat-buffets full of grain and other plant food to feed animals, who then convert it into much less food to be consumed. For every one kilogram of animal food produced, livestock are fed about six kilograms of plant food.[44] The United States livestock population consumes more than seven times as much grain as is consumed directly by the entire American population—enough to feed the entire human population of the country five times over.[45] When you see a meal with meat, what you don't see is the twelve plates of soy, corn, and other foods that are wasted, essentially thrown in the garbage, for every one plate of animal products.

Every year, close to six million children will die of starvation. Millions of tons of soybeans, maize, sunflower, rapeseed (canola), sorghum, and barley are grown and then wasted on farm animals. In 2011, there was a record harvest of over 2.5 billion tons of grains. Half of it was squandered on livestock. Seventy-seven percent of all course grain was fed to animals that produced meat, dairy, and eggs instead of feeding the malnourished.[46] When we tell our children not to waste food, a plant-based diet is the best example of how not to misuse excess food and preserve enough for everyone.

The amount of grains feed to US livestock is sufficient to feed about 840 million people who follow a plant-based diet.[47] Meanwhile, an estimated 854 million people around the world remain undernourished.[48] It is startling how similar these numbers are. Of course, there are distribution and geo-political issues that complicate the crisis, but this is a large piece of the complex world-hunger puzzle that must be taken into account.

Philip Wollen is an Australian philanthropist who climbed the corporate ladder, was named among *Australian Business Magazine*'s top-forty headhunted executives, and was formerly the vice president of CitiBank. Then, at the age of forty, he had a profound change of heart, became a vegetarian, and began to dedicate his life to helping over five hundred charities who aid animals, the homeless, the terminally ill, children, and the elderly. He argued eloquently in the *Intelligence Squared* series of debates for 2012 on the topic "Animals Should Be off the Menu." Mr. Wollen said, "As I travel around the world, I see poor countries who sell their grain to the west while their own children starve in their arms, and the west feeds it to livestock so we can eat animals. Believe me, every morsel of meat we eat is slapping the tearstained face of a hungry child."[49]

Because eating animal products, even "alternative" products, accounts for vastly greater environmental impact than consuming plant foods, eating animals amounts to an inequitable consumption of resources. It is a betrayal to our planet and an assault on the rights of others, both at present and for future generations, when we don't meet their needs for clean air, water, and other resources necessary for sustaining life. We are betraying our contract with the Earth by supporting an excessively destructive practice that is completely unnecessary—consuming meat, dairy, and eggs.

Reducing or eliminating the consumption of animal products is one of the most powerful ways we can reduce our impact on the environment. Animal products are a luxury—a lavish meal that the Earth can no longer afford. We must start thinking and acting beyond convenience and tradition and evolve to be honorable global citizens, concerned for the state of the environment and the well-being of our children worldwide. A plant-based diet is by far the most positive ecological choice we can make.

Chapter 6
Is Alternative Animal Production Sustainable?

Animals are, like us, endangered species on an endangered planet, and we are the ones who are endangering them, it, and ourselves. They are innocent sufferers in a hell of our making.

—Jeffrey Moussaieff Masson
and Susan McCarthy, *When Elephants Weep*

Visit any natural foods store and you will see a variety of terminology describing a "new way" of raising farmed animals with supposedly more eco-minded methods: local, organic, sustainable, etc. While it is certainly grounds for optimism to see that the environmental and ethical impact of our diet is increasingly affecting our collective awareness, we should pause to question: How "green" is this new meat? Is it really going to solve the numerous ecological problems of raising and killing farmed animals for their meat, milk, and eggs, or is it *greenwashing*—a marketing strategy that makes consumers think that buying a product with an eco-label will help protect the planet, when that assumption is actually false.

While sustainable, free-range beef and dairy cows might not be gobbling up quite as much grain, they are drinking notably more water than their factory-farmed brethren, because they are more active. As by-products of their metabolism, they are still producing dangerous greenhouse gasses like methane and nitrous oxide; and it takes vast amounts of land to graze these animals, space that was once habitat to wildlife and endangered species. A closer look at the production and distribution mechanisms behind alternative animal products reveals that they are not the green superstars many in the local and slow food movement believe them to be.

Local Buzz

When we think of eating green, often people think of locally produced food as being the best ecological choice. Local eating is the latest eco-buzz. Folks want to know how green their tomato is. Is it an island hopper with pages of stamps in its passport, or is it a down-home local from the farmers' market?

Local eating is the latest craze in the ever-increasing trend of being eco-conscious, but how green is it really? A paper published by George Mason University investigated the validity of *food miles*—the new term for how far your food had to travel to reach your plate—and had this to say,

> The evidence presented suggests that food miles are, at best, a marketing fad that frequently and severely distorts the environmental impacts of agricultural production. At worst, food miles constitute a dangerous distraction from the

very real and serious issues that affect energy consumption and the environmental impact of modern food production.[1]

Buying and eating regionally can be a principled pursuit; however, few people realize that in terms of eating carbon consciously, choosing a tomato is *always* a better option than choosing an animal product, regardless of the proximity of its production. While buying regionally grown and produced food is often good for decreasing greenhouse gas emissions, choosing a plant-based product over an animal product reduces our environmental impact significantly more than any consideration placed on food miles. Upon deeper investigation into production, local animal products have far more environmental impact than a tomato with a tropical tan.

Just as buying locally does not necessarily mean buying humanely, supporting local operations also offers no guarantee of sustainability. A study in the *Journal of Environmental Science and Technology* found that shifting just two meals a week from meat and dairy products to a vegan diet reduces more greenhouse gasses than buying all locally sourced food.[2] It turns out there is more to assessing the ecological consequence of a food product than where it was grown or produced. The total production effect, as well as the energy and water needed to produce the product, are far more impactful factors that must be taken into account.[3] When gauging the carbon footprint of food, transportation (how far the food traveled) is only 11 percent of the equation, while production is a stunning 83 percent.[4] And animal products are incredibly intensive on production, many times more than plant foods. Researchers using a Life Cycle Assessment (LCA) can calculate the impact of a food from *seed to plate* for plant food or *inception to plate* for animal products. Their calculations are finding again and again that animal products have a much higher impact on the environment regardless of whether they are "local," "sustainable," or otherwise.

Animals that are raised for meat, dairy, and eggs are fed soy, oats, alfalfa, and corn, among other foods. These feed crops are usually not grown locally. Even "grass-fed" cows are often fed imported grain some portion of the year when weather is not conducive to grazing, and often in the last weeks or months before slaughter to fatten them up. Grain that could be going directly to people is shipped for hundreds, sometimes thousands, of miles to feed chickens turkeys, pigs, goats, and cows that will ultimately be labeled "local."[5] This waste is in addition to the water and land wasted in growing those grains, the water the animals drank, and the fossil fuel squandered on the slaughtering process, refrigeration, etc. The energy used for production of local animal products is enormous compared to the much-lower carbon footprint of growing plants.

Indeed, smaller operations can be more environmentally damaging than larger operations that have the resources to demand higher efficiency, are able to produce more product with less input of energy, and can be much more efficient when it comes to transportation. Smaller operations use smaller vehicles that do not carry nearly as much product, and therefore the ratio of fuel usage to product transported will not always be as great as in the case of a truck that hauls much larger loads. The impact here may be on a case-by-case basis, but it is important to realize that food miles form just a small portion of the carbon footprint of any food product. Consuming plant products that are low on the food chain is the best way to ensure that your environmental footprint is green.

It is also not necessarily true that local industry is more economically beneficial than other types of industry, which may provide higher wages and better benefits to employees and may provide significant economic benefit to a community by having lower prices. While this certainly is not always the case, it is important to remember that local does not always equate to better. This issue must be examined on a case-by-case basis.

Grass-Fed Beef

Although it is often thought of as the eco-alternative to commercial red meat, the grass is really no greener for grass-feed beef. Contrary to popular belief, grass-fed beef can produce 50 to 60 percent *more* greenhouse gas emissions than their grain-eating cousins. This is due to the extended rumination of bacteria in the digestion of cellulose-rich roughage, like grass, as opposed to the relatively quick processing of grains rich in simple sugars.[6, 7] This results in grass-fed animals producing about four times more methane emissions than feedlot cattle.[8] Grass-fed or pasture raised animals also require more water, because they have a higher activity level and spend more time in the sun, especially during the summer months. Let's not forget about the rolling acres of grass these cattle feast on. Unless it's an organic operation, this grass is doused in chemical insecticides and pesticides, and organic or not, that much foliage requires massive amounts of water, often pulled from quickly drying aquifers.

With grass-fed beef, it can take eighteen to twenty-four months longer to get an animal up to market weight, because they are able to exercise and eat a more natural diet. That greatly extends the amount of time they are alive—burping greenhouse gasses, drinking our clean water and creating pollution—compared to conventional production, in which the animals can take as little as twelve months to reach market weight. Dr. Jude Capper, an assistant professor of dairy sciences at Washington State University, conducted a comprehensive comparison of conventional (feedlot) cattle, natural (feedlot finished with no growth-enhancing technology) cattle, and grass-fed (forage-fed) cattle. She found that to produce a set quantity of beef, the conventional feedlot product required the fewest animals, the least land, water, and fossil fuels and that it produced the least greenhouse gasses. Dr. Capper stated, "There's a perception out there that grass-fed animals are frolicking in the sunshine, kicking their heels up full of joy and pleasure. What we actually found was from the land-use basis, from the energy, from water, and particularly, based on the carbon footprints, grass-fed is far worse than corn-fed."[9]

Most of the new buzzword labels researched for this book were deceiving in that the environmental improvement was negligible, but the label of grass-fed beef was actually far more deceptive when compared to commercial production, as it ultimately caused more damage to the planet. James McWilliams, author of *Just Food: Where Locavores Get It Wrong and How We Can Truly Eat Responsibly*, says (of going from conventional feedlot ranching to grass-fed production), "no study I've seen convincingly shows that the exchange is worth it."[10]

Spaced Out

Another popular alternative touted as sustainable is the "free-range" (or "pasture-raised") system that rejects the intensive indoor confinement of factory farming and allegedly offers the animals a more natural existence outdoors. However, as we learned previously, many of these operations still tightly confine animals, simply opening a door in the building to a small, uninviting, concrete outdoor space and calling it "free-range." But let's assume for a moment that all the producers that use these labels are actually giving the animals even a minimal amount of space to experience a degree of a normal life. It is simply impossible to allocate sufficient land to pasture-raise animals and feed the billions of people on the planet a steady diet of meat, dairy, and eggs. At current consumption levels, to feed almost seven billion people animal products, we have to cram farmed animals into tiny spaces and stack them on top of each other. Fifty-five billion land animals are raised and slaughtered each year worldwide—that's almost eight times the number of the entire human population of the earth. They already occupy 80 percent of the Earth's total usable arable land.[11] How much more can be spared?

Whenever there is a transition to a truly free-range system, the same amount of animals will now use several more acres of land.[12] Of all the land in the United States being utilized for agriculture, 78 percent is used to raise livestock. At any given time, there are one hundred million head of cattle and seventy million pigs alive in the United States. Currently, only about 3 percent of cattle and pigs are pasture-raised and only 9 percent of all livestock.[13] How would we ever have the land to pasture-raise them all? To give all farmed animals the space they need to have even a semblance of a natural life, we would have to destroy millions more acres of wild areas, forests, prairies, and wetlands to accommodate them.

Imagine a modern egg operation, with a hundred thousand hens crowded into windowless warehouses, occupying one single acre of land. Now imagine how much land would be needed to let every single one of those hens have the room that she needs to express natural behaviors. Depending on how you define "reasonable space," that would take many times the acreage. Even simply doubling the space would not be sufficient. For these animals to be able to reestablish their natural activities such as nesting, scratching, dust-bathing, and to prevent behavioral problems such as severe feather pecking,[i] it would take several times the current acreage that is allotted for these animals. We simply don't have the space to allow all of our farmed animals the area they need to establish their natural behaviors and therefore live any sort of humane life.

We are living in an era of mass extinction. The earth has seen extinction events before, but those were due to natural causes. The current catastrophic rate of extinction is 100 percent caused by humans. Every year, thirty thousand animals go extinct. Each day, eighty-two species disappear forever. Much of this loss is due to what we choose to put on our plates, and it could be prevented with a few simple changes to our diets.[14]

Loss of biodiversity and habitat destruction are of considerable concern when it comes to animal agriculture. Globally, livestock production is one of the leading causal factors in the loss of biodiversity and a key factor in the loss of species. Within certain regions in the United States, livestock grazing is the number-one cause of species being federally listed as threatened or endangered.[15] Shifting to a diet with local animal products has the potential to *increase* the damage to biodiversity, as more communities' open spaces would be required for free-ranging animals to meet our society's demand for animal-derived foods.[16]

A study called *Rethinking Global Biodiversity Strategies*, conducted by the Netherlands Environmental Assessment Agency, looked at policy options for reversing biodiversity loss and found that a diet with no meat would have the greatest benefit on preserving

---

i Some chickens will peck at and remove feathers from another bird when they are kept in too close proximity to each other. This can lead to skin trauma and bleeding that, in turn, can cause suffering and death. This is the reason that almost all poultry operations elect to debeak the birds, a very painful procedure that has been described already in previous chapters.

plant species and wildlife. They recommend a national reduction of meat consumption.[17] Another study from the Netherlands investigated land use by the animal-agriculture sector in their country and reported that, "by using an integrated assessment model, we found a global food transition to less meat, or even a complete switch to plant-based food to have a dramatic effect on land use. Up to 2,700 Mha (hectare meters) of pasture and 100 Mha of cropland could be abandoned, resulting in a large carbon uptake from regrowing vegetation. Additionally, methane and nitrous oxide emission would be reduced substantially."[18] Livestock exclusion—removing cows from the land, streams, and waterways—has consistently resulted in the most dramatic and rapid rates of ecosystem recovery.[19]

In an interview with Joel Salatin, a sustainable animal farmer made infamous in the film *Food, Inc.* for slitting the throats of chickens on camera, he referred to his cows and confessed, "We move them every day from paddock to paddock and only give them access to a single spot a couple of days a year." Wow. How many acres does he need to be "sustainable"? He may be able to feed a few hipster foodies that seek out local animal products this way, but try to feed free-range animals to seven billion hungry people with an ever-increasing appetite for meat. It can't be done.

What Mr. Salatin is referring to in the above quote is known as *rotational grazing* or sometimes called management intensive grazing. Often touted as the eco-friendly way of raising animals for food, the argument is that the animal manure is evenly distributed as they are moved from pasture to pasture, fertilizing the grass. But what the supporters of rotational grazing are not taking into account is that this method requires a vast amount of land for a small herd of animals. There is simply not enough space for this to be our primary method of raising farmed animals.

However, that is not the only problem with this system. When animals are confined, even in a large area, they are not moving as a natural herd of ruminants would over miles and miles, so they concentrate in comfortable areas, pooping in streams and under shade trees, not evenly distributing their waste at all. To counter this quandary, some producers crowd the cattle tighter in smaller paddocks. This, however, can lead to overgrazing, trampling, and soil *pugging*. Pugging is when the ground, mixed with water and the heavy pounding of animal hooves, becomes a thick muck as much as eighteen inches deep. The soil is then less able to absorb the waste, is not sequestering carbon, and any benefits that the rotational grazer thought he was offering are negated.[20] James McWilliams, author of *Just Food*, concludes in a blog post about this dilemma, "pragmatically speaking, the environmental benefits of rotational grazing are more theoretical and rhetorical than real."[21]

A free-range steer requires two to twenty acres of land to support his growth, depending on what he is fed. Two or so acres is the minimum if he is grazing on grass. More acres would be required to grow crops like soy or corn to feed him. Even two acres is an excessive amount of land wasted on one animal. There are millions of cows currently packed onto factory farms. Envision giving each of those animals just the minimum two acres required to achieve a semblance of a natural, comfortable life. There is not enough land on the planet, or even two planets, to free-range all the millions of cows currently being raised for food. And this is just the cows. If all animals raised for food—the billions of pigs, sheep, turkeys, ducks, and chickens—were included, we would need closer to five planet Earths.[22] It simply cannot be done. Free-ranging animals for food can never be more than a niche market for a few elite buyers.

However, those two acres could be used to grow hundreds of pounds of plant food—fifteen times more food than you would get from one cow's flesh.[23] Free-range animal farming is not an ecologically viable method of food production. A global shift to a plant-based diet is the only solution to preserving our environment and having enough food to feed everyone.

Organic

The word *organic* when applied to animal agriculture is the only one of the many alternative-animal-product buzzwords that actually has some significant regulation and oversight. The animals are fed a diet free of pesticides and genetic engineering, and they are not given pharmaceuticals or antibiotics. They are also given access to the outdoors, although in some cases, especially with poultry, this could just be an open door or window to an unappealing gravel patio.

The animals' feed is organic; however, nearly all the other detrimental environmental impacts of animal agriculture still apply to organic animal products. The animals are still emitting greenhouse gases from their belching, flatulence, and mountains of concentrated excrement. They are still drinking excessively, and water is still being wasted to grow the organic grain to feed them. They are still contributing to soil depletion and topsoil erosion. They still use unnecessary fossil fuel, and they are still using large areas of land, especially if the animals have access to the outside—which is a requirement of the organic label. All of these impacts could be significantly reduced by replacing the consumption of animal products with plant products.

A study of Swedish organic meat found that organic pork production actually created more nitrogen oxide and other greenhouse gas emissions than conventional pork production.

Emissions were slightly lower for cow and lamb production; however, the land use was higher, limiting its sustainability and offsetting the other advantages.[24]

Another study found that organic milk production lowered the *eutrophication* potential to waterways due to the reduced fertilizer use. Eutrophication is the biological reaction when excessive nutrients (from pesticides and excrement) stimulate the growth of primary producers like algae, which deplete water of oxygen and create a toxic environment for aquatic life. However, the study found that organic milk production significantly increases land use and methane emissions, so again, the harm negates the gains.[25]

According to a study commissioned by Germany's foodwatch organization, producing beef and milk organically actually increased greenhouse gas emissions in some cases, and the reduction for other animals raised organically was minimal. The study states that shifting from a conventional diet that includes meat and dairy to an organic diet of the same reduces emissions by 8 percent. Yet switching from a conventional animal-product diet to a conventional vegan diet reduces emissions by 87 percent. And the ultimate in reduction, a 100 percent organic, vegan diet, reduces emissions by a whopping 94 percent.[26]

The benefit of organic animal agriculture is not enough to warrant its existence and certainly not enough to tout it as a solution to our current environmental crisis. When comparing organic animal products to fruit and vegetable production, we find the difference is startling. Plant-based foods cause far less environmental impact than organic animal products.

Polyface Farms is a poster-child alternative animal operation, and its owner, Joel Salatin, writes books on how to raise animals non-conventionally—and how to kill them. In one section of his book *Folks, This Ain't Normal*, he effectively admits that vegetable farming is better than raising animals:

> We have a huge garden at Polyface Farm. We love our vegetables and so should you. As I see it, the advantage of vegetables is that they can be grown in tiny spaces. Highly productive per square foot, they allow us to leverage small areas in proximity to where we live and work. They don't have to be fenced in like animals; they don't make any noise; they don't poop. A little area goes a long way with vegetables. We could literally grow all the vegetables we need in this country simply by using our backyards, roads edges, and vacant urban lots.

The desire to seek out ecologically sustainable, green food products is a monumental step in the right direction, which animal agribusiness is attempting to exploit. The advantages of alternative animal production are extremely minimal and, in some cases, are actually more detrimental for the environment. Eating meat is a culturally ingrained habit that our society clings to even as it impedes our progress and our future on the planet. It is understandable that many believe the rhetoric that sustainable animal products exist, and if we just pay a little more, we can still enjoy what we are used to—all while helping the planet. Unfortunately, this is a myth. Animal agriculture simply cannot be done on a scale that will feed the world and still allow the planet to recover. We must shift our behavior and enjoy the abundant, delicious plant-based options our world offers if we wish to leave our children a livable planet.

Choosing plant foods over animal foods is always the more ecologically sound choice, no matter how the animal was raised. Let's create a world where the diverse species are protected, the water and air are sweet and clean, the soil is healthy, and we no longer directly kill and destroy for our food. Eating an organic plant-based diet is truly eating green and one of the most powerful things you can do to decrease your carbon footprint, reduce suffering, and live a vibrant, healthy life.

Chapter 7
Deadstock

Death is a mystery, and burial is a secret.

— Stephen King, *Pet Sematary*

What the heck is deadstock? No, it's not a Grateful Dead reunion in upstate New York. In animal agriculture, deadstock refers to the approximately 60 percent of the animal that cannot be used after slaughter, as well as animals that die before they reach the slaughterhouse. Deadstock is equally a problem in commercial and alternative production; there are millions of animal carcasses to dispose of in any production method. After the choice cuts are separated from the body, the bones, tendons, ligaments, entrails, plasma, sphincters, hooves, hair, feathers, etc. are waste that must be disposed of, as they cannot be used for consumption. Animals that are killed or die from illness, accident, or injury before they make it to the slaughterhouse must also be disposed of as they cannot legally be used for consumption. Disease outbreaks can cause mass killings on a farm, with tens of thousands of animal carcasses that cannot be processed into food as a result.[1] One pork facility with a "one thousand sow farrow-to-finish" (i.e.

birth to death) capacity will have about twenty tons of dead pigs a year.[2] For the industry as a whole, these billions of tons of potentially toxic waste are as much of an environmental concern as the animals were when alive—belching methane and wasting resources.[3]

The livestock industry in the United States produces billions of tons of waste each year. Much of that is deadstock. Previously, this animal waste material went to animal-rendering plants, where it was processed into raw material and gelatin for everything from cosmetics to pet food to candles to crayons. However, most was used for livestock feed; ground-up animals were fed to other animals. This forced cannibalization for herbivorous animals led to BSE (bovine spongiform encephalopathy), or "mad cow disease," first discovered in 1986.[4] With the discovery of this deadly disease, the practice of rendering became strongly controlled, with costly regulations, and was finally banned in 1997. Limiting the use of the material for livestock feed eliminated one of the rendering facilities' biggest demands and has hurt the rendering industry, which has had to close factory doors across the United States.

In 2009, the FDA required that the brains and spinal cords of cows older than thirty months must be removed and disposed of, further burdening rendering plants. The intention of this action was to keep the prions, the parts of the nervous system that could contain mad cow disease, from entering any product that could be ingested, but the cost to the rendering industry has been great. They have been forced to conglomerate into fewer operations as the cost of rendering has gone up five-fold.[5]

Burial

Slaughterhouses and processing plants are often left with no alternative but to find ways to dispose of the unusable waste themselves. An increasingly popular method of disposal is creating mass graves; this is sometimes called trench burial. The rancher or slaughterhouse will dig massive trenches and bulldoze tens of thousands of pounds of dead animal parts into them. Some states require permits to do this, and some do not. Some states require a minimal depth and covering material, and some do not. This is quite literally a case of sweeping unwanted waste under the rug, and the environmental impact is enormous. Groundwater poisoning and pollution has been documented at the burial site and downstream. It can take up to twenty-five years for a carcass to decompose. In the meantime, the leaching of chlorine, ammonium, nitrate, coliforms, *E. coli* and other bacteria, water borne protozoa, and the bovine spongiform encephalopathy (BSE, or mad cow disease) agent intensifies with rainfall and pollutes groundwater for decades.[6] There is also the concern of scavenger animals digging up the remains and creating an unsightly public health hazard.

Disposal Pits

A similar method of slow decomposition is disposal pits. These are massive above-ground boxes with solid walls and coverings, and carcasses are continuously added. One environmental advantage to the disposal pit is a reduction of toxins leaching into the water table. However, this method produces malodorous gasses, such as methane and carbon dioxide from the decomposing corpses, contributing to climate change. The estimated gaseous makeup emitted during decomposition of a carcass would be approximately 45 percent carbon dioxide, 35 percent methane, 10 percent nitrogen, with the remainder comprised of traces of other gasses, such as hydrogen sulfide.[7] Disposal pits can also produce hydrogen sulfite exceeding human safety levels.[8] Numerous scientific studies show that these methods of dead animal dumping can create leaching and gases for up to twenty years after disposal[9] not to mention a horrible stench assaulting any nose within a few mile radius.

Incineration

Incineration, or burning the deadstock, has its own set of significant environmental problems. Pyres of animal corpses, which are usually burned in oil inside converted gas tanks, release sulfur dioxide, carbon monoxide, nitrogen oxide, and heavy metals into the atmosphere, contributing to global warming and acid rain. These toxins can easily reach the human food and water supply as well.[10] If an animal is diseased, that disease can become airborne and spread. Incineration is a poor solution, with a host of environmental and health concerns.

Composting Cadavers

Another method of disposal that is growing in popularity is composting the cadavers of animals. The bodies are thrown into a large bin with other organic matter and composted down to make fertilizer. While this sounds innocuous on the surface, there are issues with composting, as well. One is that bones and horns don't break down quickly, and the rancher can soon find that he has more dead bodies than space to compost them. A more harmful problem—beyond the hide, horns, entrails, and bones—is that other materials being processed are antibiotics, growth promoters, vaccines, and an array of chemicals routinely used in animal agriculture (unless it is a certified organic operation). The finished compost is a toxic soup. States that allow the use of this material limit its application to projects like highway landscaping.

Digesters

Another way to deal with slaughterhouse waste is through technology that facilitates anaerobic digestion. The digesters convert the waste into biogas, a mixture of carbon dioxide and methane that can be converted into usable energy. But digesters come with their own set of concerns. The cost of building and running a digester is enormous, and they are water intensive, as well. Additionally, they produce wastewater sludge that must then be disposed of properly. Like composting, the final product is practically unusable as fertilizer due to the toxicity levels, not to mention the prions and heat-resistant bacteria that are not eliminated in the digestion process. Furthermore, digesters do a poor job of breaking down long-chain fatty acids, leaving behind a thick layer of greasy, useless fat at the end of digestion that must also be disposed of. Finally, digesters are not practical, because they have to be constructed far from residential areas due to bio-security and odor problems.[11]

With rendering plants on the decline, and other solutions to the slaughterhouse waste problem fraught with environmental hazards, it is time to start talking about the deadstock dilemma with the same level of concern as the environmental impact of livestock. This is yet another powerful reason to reduce our dependence on animal products, irrespective of the production method, and embrace ecologically safe plant-based eating.

Chapter 8
The Ultimate Betrayal of Our Oceans

We must stop eating the oceans. Eating fish is, for all intents and purposes, an ecological crime.

—Captain Paul Watson, Sea Shepherd

The planet may never recover from the environmental devastation wrought by commercial fishing. It seems that our oceans, once thought to hold an endless bounty, are no match for insatiable human greed. Many fish species that were once considered infinitely numerous are in grave danger of being hunted to extinction. The ocean is not the renewable resource it was once thought to be, and there are just too many people on earth for seafood to be a sustainable food choice.

Billions of fish worldwide are killed for food every year. Scientists predict that, unless current fishing rates are drastically reduced, *every* species of wild-caught seafood will collapse by the year 2050.[1, 2] Excessive fish depletion can widely be attributed to advances in fishing technology and techniques, coupled with minimal regulations, restrictions, and lack of enforcement of the rules that are in place to allow fish to repopulate. Technologies like sonar, charting equipment, and spotter aircraft with temperature mapping all make humans a terrifying predator. There is no ocean deep enough to hide from the rapacious destroyer that is the modern fishing industry.

Large computerized ships trawl the deep seas with miles of netting that can obliterate 130 tons of fish in a single sweep.[3] Bottom trawlers cause massive destruction, scraping the sea bottom and destroying miles of coral, sponges, and non-target bottom-dwelling fish, which are then simply discarded as collateral damage.

In fact, fishing is one of the world's most wasteful and destructive industries. Every year, more than seven million tons of so-called by-catch (perhaps more accurately described as by-kill) is inadvertently caught and wantonly destroyed, including over three hundred thousand sea animals such as non-target fish species, sea turtles, dolphins, whales, sharks, albatrosses, and other sea birds.[4, 5] Every year over seven million tons of marine life are caught unintentionally by the fishing industry just to be callously thrown back dead; this is considered an acceptable loss in the industrial hunger for profit.[6] A 2005 study showed that for every five pounds of fish caught in US commercial fisheries, one pound is dumped overboard, dead or dying.[7]

All seventeen of the world's major fishing estuaries are overfished. The 2008 *State of World Fisheries and Aquaculture* report released by the Food and Agriculture Organization (FAO) of the United Nations concludes that 80 percent of all marine fish stocks are currently fully exploited, overexploited, or depleted, including stocks of the seven largest prey fisheries. Nearly 90 percent of all large predatory fish in the ocean are now gone, forcing nations to increasingly fish lower on the food webs to meet seafood demands.[8] Fishermen are having to voyage farther out, deploy more nets, and stay out on the water longer in order to catch fewer and fewer fish.

Because of human exploitation of the oceans, endangered species are left starving, or they end up helplessly fighting for life, caught in fishing nets that kill indiscriminately. As humans we have a choice in what we eat. Marine mammals are not so fortunate; they need fish to live, and we are in effect stealing and annihilating their only means of sustenance.

Endangered species are also vulnerable to industry nets and other gear. Whales not only face the threat of Japanese and Icelandic whaling, but deep-sea fishing trawlers are proving to be even more dangerous. By-catch was found to be the biggest threat to whales by the US Commission on Ocean Policy in 2004,[9] and little has changed. The International Whaling Commission estimates that three hundred thousand cetaceans (whales, dolphins, and porpoises) are killed by fishing nets and gear every year.[10] Just as the dolphins are trapped and die in the tuna-industry nets, sea turtles are killed by the millions in the nets of the shrimping industry. In fact, for every pound of shrimp netted in the Gulf of Mexico, four pounds of by-kill is wasted and thrown back overboard, dead.[11] Most people would never consider eating an endangered sea turtle, but eating shrimp directly causes sea turtles to be further threatened.

Many of us are familiar with the television show *Whale Wars* and the brave activists of Sea Shepherd, who embark on perilous and courageous journeys each season, fighting to protect the majestic whales in the Antarctic Sea. But Sea Shepherd recognizes the plight of other critical creatures in the ocean and has ships in the Mediterranean protecting bluefin tuna, as well. Bluefin tuna are large, torpedo-shaped, warm-blooded fish that can reach speeds up to forty-five miles an hour. They are endangered, and due to overfishing for sushi and canning, nearing extinction—if intervention is not swift. The bluefin is a vital link in the fragile marine ecosystem and the catch has declined by 80 percent in the last twenty years.[12] How tragic that valiant activists must risk their lives to defend this important species when the solution is so simple—vegan sushi, anyone?

We are depleting the oceans of fish at an alarming rate, fish intended not only for human consumption but also for animal consumption. Half the world's fish catch is ultimately fed to livestock. In fact, more fish are consumed by US livestock than by the entire human population of all the countries of Western Europe combined.[13] Ninety percent of small pelagic (ocean) fish, such as anchovies, sardines, and menhaden, are ground up into fish meal and oil, and approximately a third of that is fed to livestock. When we take massive amounts of small fish from the ocean to fatten up our farmed animals, we are leaving larger ocean dwellers like tuna, salmon, and seabirds with empty bellies, and they are starving to death. Pigs and chickens are eating more fish than sharks and seagulls—and not only in commercial operations but in alterative production as well. What an absolute waste.

There is new evidence that depleting our oceans is hastening global warming, adding even further evidence of the marine ecosystem's global importance. A study in the prestigious journal *Science* found that fish droppings help the ocean absorb carbon dioxide. Alkaline chemicals, such as calcium carbonate in fish excrement, balance acidity in the oceans and help take CO_2 out of the atmosphere.[14] With massive depletion of fish, and corresponding diminishing supply of fish poop, the oceans are unable to capture the CO_2 as they have been doing for millennia. The global-warming effect is raising sea temperatures and sea levels, causing the acidification of the ocean, and destroying coral, plankton, and other marine life.

Fish Farming

About half of the fish consumed in the United States are caught in the wild and half are farmed.[15] Fish farming, or aquaculture, is not an acceptable alternative to the devastation caused to the ocean by commercial fishing. Just as when land animals are confined in animal agriculture, the same problems arise when large numbers of fish are concentrated in small tanks—they get sick from the overcrowded, unnatural, stressful conditions, and produce concentrated, ecologically dangerous waste.

In aquaculture, tens of thousands of fish swim in a tank about the size of a swimming pool, which becomes a filthy cesspool of their own excrement. Fish farms are notorious for dumping an arsenal of chemicals into the tanks, as well as antibiotics and other pharmaceuticals. Concentrated fish feces, dead fish, uneaten food, feed additives, coloring agents, algaecides, zinc, copper, paints, and disinfectants all mix in these polluted waters and leach into the surrounding groundwater. The seafloor under fish farms has increased nitrogen and toxin levels.[16] The farms also pose a threat to the surviving wild fish outside the tanks. Farmed salmon occasionally escape by the millions and introduce diseases to wild salmon.[17]

Fish farms use wild fish to feed their farmed fish, so the industry ends up killing more fish than it produces. Producing a pound of farmed salmon requires three pounds of wild-caught fish.[18] An Inter-American Tropical Tuna Commission study revealed that up to sixty million metric tons of "harvested wild fish" per year are required to feed the three million tons of the three major tropical tuna species that we are now harvesting annually from fish farms. As in the production of land animals, the fish-farming industry is incredibly wasteful.

Shrimp Farming

Shrimp is one of the most popular seafood dishes in the United States, and most people would assume that it has a lower carbon footprint than beef. But that is not the case when it comes to much of the shrimp produced by aquaculture. According to a University of Oregon study, farmed shrimp in Southeast Asia had a carbon footprint ten times larger than cattle raised on land that was once rainforest.

Acres of picturesque coastal mangrove forests are destroyed to create shrimp farms in Latin America and Asia. The mangrove's soil is rich with carbon, which is released into the atmosphere when the trees are cut. Not only is carbon released, but critical habitats for birds and wildlife are destroyed, and yet more ecological problems are created. These farms are only productive for about five years before the build-up of sludge in the water is so great that the shrimp can no longer live, due to the acidic soil. After serving their temporary purpose, these once-magnificent forests are trashed and abandoned as sludge-filled wastelands.

The study concluded that due to this forest destruction, 100 grams of shrimp represented over 436 pounds of carbon dioxide. That is the equivalent of burning almost 20 gallons of gasoline. The carbon footprint of shrimp killed on a farm from deforested mangroves is ten times more than that of beef from cows killed on land from deforested rainforest. Over 90 percent of shrimp consumed in the United States is imported; it comes mostly from Asia.[19]

"Sustainably Caught" Labeling

Some groceries and fish markets now offer fish and shellfish labeled with a variety of labels indicating sustainability, including the most popular, a certification from the Marine Stewardship Council (MSC) with a blue label stating "Certified Sustainable Seafood." Consumers are led to believe that these labels guarantee the fish were obtained by ecologically sensitive means, but scientists and critics are warning that this is simply an elaborate case of greenwashing.

To grant any sustainability labeling, generally the auditors are looking to see if the target fish population is healthy and that the by-catch has as minimal an impact as possible (it is impossible not to kill non-target species). Finally, they look at the management practices of the company. The degree and level of what is considered sustainable differs from label to label, and checking for compliance is a difficult endeavor, as an inspector has to accompany the vessel out to sea to assure respect for the rules. This happens on only a fraction of the voyages.

Environmentalists who are evaluating the systems of compliance for labeling say that the standards are not high enough to really make any significant or long-term improvements. In 2006, Walmart agreed to buy MSC–certified fish as a sizeable amount of their fish sold, and critics have said that to meet the demands of this massive account, MSC's standards have dropped even farther.

A prime example of MSC's misconduct with their labeling can be found off the coast of Nova Scotia and concerns the long-line fishing of swordfish. Long-line fishing, like net trawling, is another indiscriminate fishing method that kills many more fish species than the intended target. A long-line is a lengthy procession of hooks on a fishing line that can be forty to fifty miles in length. Swordfisherman know that when they go out for their catch, they will also be killing many other fish, including sharks. In fact, for every one swordfish, two endangered blue sharks are caught on the line. The swordfishing industry "accidentally" kills tens of thousands of sharks every year.[20] Swordfish numbers are stable for now, but this fishing practice violates the second principle of the sustainable labeling, excessive by-kill of a sensitive species. The MSC has chosen to ignore this problem, offering Nova Scotia swordfish their seal of approval and selling most of their sustainably labeled swordfish to Whole Foods in the United States.

Scientist and environmentalists are seeing this kind of violation of consumer trust with many of the "sustainably caught" labels and are concerned that people think they are helping the oceans with their fish purchases, when there is simply not enough fish to meet current seafood demands worldwide and remain sustainable. It just can't be done.

Shark Finning

As a top predator species, sharks play an integral role in the ocean ecosystem. There are over five hundred species of sharks, whose fossil record dates back over 420 million years, making them one of the most ancient fish species. Although extremely successful, having survived four great cycles of extinction, including the last great extinction ending the age of the dinosaurs, sharks are now facing their most dangerous threat in millions of years: human predation. In the last few decades, the population of nearly every species of large shark has dramatically declined due to the global demand for shark-fin soup. In this dish, the tasteless fin is included only to provide a much-coveted texture; shark fin provides no flavor of its own. Mostly consumed in China, Hong Kong, and

Taiwan, this opulent dish, once enjoyed only by emperors and nobility, has experienced an explosion of popularity in modern times as incomes in China increase.

The demand for shark fin soup has created a brutal trade akin to that of elephant ivory or rhino horn through a fishing practice called shark finning. Shark finning involves the removal of the dorsal fin, side fins, and sometimes the tail. The sharks frequently survive the finning, only to be thrown back into the ocean, maimed and bleeding, to suffer a cruel and ignoble death. The fatally injured sharks sink to the bottom, unable to swim, and slowly die. Shark meat itself has a decidedly lower value and lower demand than the fins, so it is rarely worth keeping the body of the shark.

Every year, as many as seventy-three million sharks are killed in this manner for shark fin soup.[21] This unnecessary dish, a sign of wealth and affluence, has been a major contributor to the near collapse of many shark species worldwide. Because sharks maintain the natural balance in our ocean's ecosystems, scientists are warning that their massive decline is having a devastating effect on the marine health and stability of systems from coral reefs to eelgrass beds. The situation is so dire that ocean nonprofit groups are forcing governments and fisheries managers to address the politically sensitive topic of banning a dish associated with an ethnic demographic, and they are scrambling to put bans on the possession, sale, and distribution of shark fins.

The US states of Hawaii, California, Washington, Oregon, and Illinois have all put bans in place on the sale and trade of shark fins. Seven other US states are considering similar legislation, and cities in Canada, the European Union, and Asia are following suit. But this, unfortunately, represents only a small fraction of the coastline areas that are importing shark fins. With 95 percent of the shark fin trade going to Asia, these efforts are making only a small difference in the overall consumption worldwide. Banning the importation of shark fins and drawing international attention to the issue—the work of Sea Stewards, Oceana, WildAid, and like organizations—is having a disproportionately small impact.

"We don't feel for sharks as we do for other animals like our furry or feathered friends," recounts David McGuire, shark conservationist and a leader in the shark fin trade movement. He goes on to say,

> We have been programmed to fear, loathe, and even hate them. But I have been in the water with sharks, including the predators of the most fearsome reputations, like tiger sharks and great white sharks. I have experienced a cognizance when diving with these sharks, an absence of malice, even a curiosity. I have also seen them struggling at the end of a hook, dead sharks bleeding on the decks and rooftops laden with drying shark fins. It's time we protect sharks for their importance to the marine ecosystem, and as beautiful animals worthy of respect alive and not just in a bowl of soup.

Fish Feel

For many people, fish and the vast number of diverse, fascinating, and often breathtakingly beautiful marine wildlife species known as "seafood" are exempted from the same ethical consideration they give to land animals. Why?

It's true they don't look like us, they aren't warm-blooded, they don't breathe as we do, but science is revealing that we can no longer use these differences to justify our callous treatment of these amazing animals. An article in the journal *Fish and Fisheries* states that, "although it may seem extraordinary to those comfortably used to prejudging animal intelligence on the basis of brain volume, in some cognitive domains fishes can even be favorably compared to nonhuman primates."[22]

Fish learn, they have complex social relationships, they care for their young, they have even been observed using tools. Many fish have a natural lifespan comparable in length to our own. It has been scientifically proven that fish have the same central nervous systems as every other vertebrate animal, including humans. When exposed to pain, fish try desperately to escape. If the pain is chronic, they show typical behavioral signs like fear, anxiety, loss of appetite, rubbing the painful area, and they are defensive—exactly the same way that mammals, reptiles, avians, and even humans act under the same circumstances. When the fish are given painkillers their behavior normalizes. And like other animals, they learn to avoid places and actions that inflict pain.[23, 24, 25]

As a result of these scientific findings, many fish farmers and anglers in the United Kingdom can face checks by inspectors from the Royal Society for Prevention of Cruelty to Animals (RSPCA) if they receive a report regarding welfare issues toward fish.[26] Many Scottish fish farmers are also being forced to heed the RSPCA's guidelines on fish welfare, from housing to transport to slaughter.

However, fish (like birds and rabbits) are not included in the Humane Methods of Slaughter Act in the United States, which affirms that an animal must be rendered unconscious before slaughter. When fish are caught, transported, and handled, they are crowded and netted, removed from the water, and hauled into boats and trucks—all stressful procedures that can cause pain, injury, and death. When brought out of the deep waters of the ocean, they suffer immense pain due to decompression. Their eyes bulge out, their swim bladders rupture, and their stomachs are sometimes pushed out their mouths. Once out of the water, they slowly suffocate or are cut up while fully conscious.

Recent studies have shown that fish, as well as crustaceans like crabs and lobsters, not only experience pain as an unpleasant stimulus to be avoided but suffer the psychological effects of pain, as well. Dr. Victoria Braithwaite of Edinburgh University states, "Recent suggestions that fish cannot experience pain or suffering do not appear to be supported by the current research. The evidence ... suggests that fish do have the capacity to experience pain and fear, and therefore we need to consider how to minimize their potential suffering."[27] Crustaceans, including lobsters, crabs, and prawns, have been found in several recent studies to meet both the behavioral and physiological criteria for feeling pain and stress.[28, 29, 30]

Mercy for Animals, an influential nonprofit organization dedicated to exposing the suffering of animals killed for food, went undercover in a Texas fish-processing facility. The investigator witnessed and documented dozens of catfish piled on top of one another in buckets, gasping and writhing, workers using pliers to peel the skin off living fish, and skinned fish still struggling and gasping on the cutting table. This is typical of the type of insensitive treatment that fish endure on their way to market, and there is not a single federal law to protect them.

"Catch and release" is a popular method of sport fishing where a fish is caught by a hook in the mouth but then thrown back in the water still alive. Even if the animal survives, the "enjoyment" of capturing a fish should not outweigh the pain and trauma caused by catch and release. Many anglers feel that they are doing no harm with catch-and-release fishing. However the Oklahoma Department of Wildlife Conservation found that as many as 43 percent of fish released after being caught on a line died within six days. The experience can be so traumatic for the fish that the stress causes a large lactic acid buildup in their muscles, which can harm their bodies and make them more susceptible to illness. They can also suffer oxygen depletion from being out of the water for an extended period of time, injuries to their mouths and throats from the hook, and damage to their scales and skin from the struggle and handling. If these impacts do not kill them, they make them more vulnerable to disease.[31] Catch and release is not the benign sport that most fishermen believe it to be.

Not a Healthy Choice

There is no physiological need for humans to eat fish. Like all meat, fish has no magical property that can only be found in its flesh. Plants provide omega-3 fatty acids and protein without the saturated fat, cholesterol, possible mercury, and heavy metals—not to mention the destruction of the oceans that surely come with a meal of fish. Plants also provide a surplus of nutrients that are lacking in any animal sources.

Eating fish is the number-one way humans become contaminated with methyl mercury. The world's leading mercury scientists have concluded that the risks posed by fish contaminated with mercury calls for a worldwide general warning to the public, especially to children and women of childbearing age.[32] Ingestion of methyl mercury is linked to cardiovascular disease, blindness, deafness, fetal brain damage, and problems with motor skills, language, and attention span. Also found in most fish are levels of PCBs, DDT, lead, dioxin, heavy metals, and a wide array of other toxins.[33, 34]

Compared to red meat, fish may have been a relatively healthy food at one time. But with all the concentrated chemicals that accumulate in their bodies, in addition to the saturated fat and cholesterol, the risk now outweighs any small potential benefits. Older, larger fish, such as tuna, are the most dangerous to human consumption, but all fish contain a certain amount of chemicals that are toxic to humans. Flaxseed oil, walnuts, and olive oil are much safer and more humane sources of omega-3s.

As the most powerful species on the plant, we have a responsibility for stewardship toward the natural world. The species that depend on us for protection are instead being destroyed by our misappropriation of power. With power comes responsibility, and in this sense we are failing in our duty as the most powerful species. We are betraying the oceans with our wanton killing and, in turn, betraying ourselves by neglecting our potential to be a great species—instead of one whose most significant legacy is to wreak destruction, death, and extinction upon others. The mysterious and remarkable ocean is in desperate peril and will soon be an empty wasteland, unless we reclaim the waters and refuse to support the mass extinction that we are currently causing. To paraphrase Capitan Paul Watson, of Sea Shepherd—what befalls the ocean befalls us all. The world is a connected web; we cannot have a healthy planet without a healthy marine ecosystem. We have a choice to make, a choice that we face three times a day. We have a responsibility to stop eating the oceans.

Chapter 9
Lab-Grown Lamb and Sci-Fi Sausage

We should all be concerned about the future, because we will have to spend the rest of our lives there.

—Charles F. Kettering

With the world population expected to top nine billion by the year 2050[1]—accompanied by an ever-increasing voracious demand for meat on the global market—scientists are looking for low-carbon ways to feed a hungry world. According to a study from the Oxford University,[2] they may find answers in lab-grown meat. In vitro meat, as it is called, has been a scientific daydream for decades, but the technology is finally catching up with the vision. Cultured commercial ground beef and sausage may be in supermarkets and on menus as soon as 2016.

According to the Oxford study, artificial meat could be produced with up to 96 percent lower greenhouse gas emissions, 99 percent lower land use, and 96 percent lower water use than conventional meat.[3] With in vitro meat we could drastically reduce the severe environmental impact of animal agriculture and abolish the need to raise and exploit animals for food.

For some, it is a bitter pill to swallow, but it is unlikely that we will reach a critical mass of people worldwide who will willingly choose to eliminate environmentally destructive animal products from their diets before catastrophic damage has been done to the planet. The unfortunate reality is that many people will continue to choose to eat meat even when presented with the hard facts: the horrible suffering of animals raised for food, the devastating environmental brunt of animal agriculture, and the ruthless reality that people are starving because of our meat-centered diets. Despite our best efforts at education, some people will still feel that it is their right and privilege to follow the whims of their palates instead of higher ethical imperatives.

Lacking the necessary shift in demand, supermarkets will not voluntarily remove animal products from their shelves and restaurants will not change their menus, but with cultured meat *they wouldn't have to.* No animals would be bred, raised, or killed for food, yet no one would have to give up meat. Because cultured meat is technically the same as conventional meat, meat eaters would not have to make what might seem to be the austere sacrifice of renouncing their dietary entitlements. In vitro meat could be an example of technology not only saving *us* but saving the animals and the environment, as well. By simultaneously indulging their traditional palatal preferences and reducing animal suffering and environmental impact, people could, quite literally, have their meat and eat it too!

According to New Harvest,[4] a nonprofit organization advancing alternatives to meat, the process of creating cultured meat begins by taking a number of cells from one living farm animal and propagating them in a nutrient-rich solution. After the cells are developed, they are grown on a biodegradable scaffold, just as vines wrapping around a trellis. In theory, a single cell could be used to feed a global population meat for a year as cultured cells keep multiplying billions of times. The end result could then be processed and cooked as boneless meat such as sausage, hamburger, or chicken nuggets. It could even be manipulated to be more nutritious and safer than the flesh of an animal with a lower percentage of saturated fat; could be infused with omega-3 fatty acids; and would certainly contain no hormones, additives, antibiotics, and other unhealthy substances, as well as being free of pathogens such as *Salmonella*, *Campylobacter*, pathogenic *E. coli*, avian influenza and bovine spongiform encephalopathy (BSE).

But is in vitro meat safe? Opponents might levy similar complaints against lab-grown meat as they do against genetically modified organisms (GMOs), but these are completely different issues. With GMOs there is the concern that modified organisms might cross-pollinate and eventually breed with, and thus permanently alter, traditional crops or even wild species. There is no such concern with in vitro meat, because entire organisms will not be produced, so these cellular cultures cannot reproduce with any animals. It will simply be like choosing a synthetic vitamin supplement over one that was extracted from a plant—completely identical and indistinguishable from the more "natural" option. To argue otherwise would be to perpetuate the naturalistic fallacy that just because something is natural it is better. By that logic we could eliminate agriculture from our lives completely, as well as artificial processes like basic hygiene, transportation, plumbing, medicine, etc.

But there is one potentially fatal flaw to all this—will consumers accept in vitro meat? There is unquestionably a "yuck" factor that will have to be overcome. However, if industries can get consumers to knowingly and willingly inhale toxic smoke from tobacco or ingest dangerous phosphoric acid in soda, then certainly this should be much easier—and more welcome. An effective marketing campaign and an equal or lower price point should easily quell these concerns. After all, how much actual meat is in those Chicken McNuggets and Whoppers anyway? It doesn't seem like much of a leap to add a little cultured meat in there, does it?

On a personal note, while meat grown in a lab may seem a little weird to some, it doesn't bother us in the least. Cogen and I like to watch sci-fi. Okay, full confession, we're addicted! Our usual fix is Star Trek, so we have been used to thinking about replicated food for years—bowl, spoon, and all. Did you know that everyone on the *Enterprise* is vegan? (we must clarify so we don't get in Trekkie trouble—we are talking about *Enterprise D*, not *NX* or *NCC 1701*, as they did not have replicator technology yet. Are our Vulcan ears showing?) Oh, they eat chicken soup, beef chili, and chocolate cake, but it is synthesized in the replicator. No animals were harmed in the making of those futuristic meals. Fictional Star Trek technology has become reality in our daily lives already (think cell phones, touch screens, and iPads), so why not replicated meat? Star Trek has been doing the marketing for us for decades.

Some may argue that there are plenty of plant-based meats already. This is true, and their existence has made it easier for many people who are willing to reduce their meat intake. However, from the obstinate perspective of a segment of the public, these products are *not* meat. People are still demanding animal protein. Lab-grown meat has the potential to provide the industry a way to solve the numerous dilemmas of meat consumption and not commit the unthinkable crime of forcing vegetarianism on an unwilling public.

If any of the dramatic advantages that cultured meat represents are going to become realities, we must take what may at first be an unpopular stance of supporting in vitro meat. The more we speak out in favor of it, the more likely we will reap the benefit to the environment that far surpasses anything that recycling, light bulbs, or electric cars can achieve. Cultured meat can end the needless misery of billions of animals used for human consumption. If we can feed more people with significantly less resources and waste, while eliminating farmed-animal suffering, let's let technology redeem itself and feed the world responsibly and compassionately.

Part 3
The Ultimate Betrayal of Our Health

Chapter 10
The Ultimate Betrayal of Our Health

Quite simply, the more you substitute plant foods for animal foods, the healthier you are likely to be.

—T. Colin Campbell, PhD

Recently, Dr. Suess's beloved children's book *The Lorax* was made into a computer-animated feature film, complete with truffula trees, the Once-ler, and the most adorable cuddly bears with gigantic, dreamy eyes. The Lorax is that mythical, mustached, annoying environmental activist who "speaks for the trees." In the movie, there is a scene where the Once-ler is appeasing the forest creatures with marshmallows. He offers one to the Lorax, who sniffs it cautiously, peers at it skeptically, and says, "I'm going to eat this, but I am highly offended by it!"

The Lorax was offended by the artificial, unhealthy, and manufactured marshmallow but uncontrollably tempted to enjoy the fluffy puff in his mouth. Most of us can relate. Marshmallows are far from a natural food and perhaps could be at the top of a list of harmful foods, yet you can now find them in vegan form.

Yes, vegan marshmallows, vegan cinnamon buns, vegan cupcakes, and vegan nacho cheese can all be purchased online and shipped directly to your home. Vegan delectables are also popping up at natural-food stores and even local bakeries and specialty shops. These alternative foods are certainly healthier than the originals that are packed with saturated fat and cholesterol from animal ingredients, but they are not entirely healthy. Twenty years ago, if you were vegan, there was a good chance that your diet was the cleanest and healthiest around, because the vegan food available was limited to vegetables, fruit, beans, and rice. If you wanted a vegan cookie, you had to bake it. Fast-forward two decades, and it's possible to be a junk-food vegan, having the majority of your diet come from vegan fast food and snack food, like vegan pizza and doughnuts.

The positive side of this explosion in vegan food manufacturing is that many more people are willing to eat less animal products if they can still indulge in vegan cupcakes and veggie hot dogs. The variety keeps it interesting, and cravings for comfort foods can be satisfied. The animals and the planet benefit, but what about our health?

Just switching from a diet of pizza and doughnuts to one of *vegan* pizza and doughnuts is not going to offer optimal health. A variety of whole grains, legumes, vegetables, and fruits must make up the majority of the diet. If people go vegan to save animals, they are taking responsibility for the welfare of other nonhuman species. It would be consistent to extend this same consideration to their own bodies. It's okay to indulge in all that the modern vegan-food world has to offer—but in reasonable quantities. Making the healthy choices our staples and practicing indulgence in moderation is critical to our health as a species and to the portrayal of veganism as a viable alternative to the current harmful practices in animal agriculture.

These vegan goodies have their place in the effort to get people to eat cruelty-free and more sustainably. When you bring a box of vegan doughnuts to the office, or bake a friend a vegan birthday cake, you are sending a message that you can eat without harming animals and still participate in all of the customs, conventions, traditions, and indulgences as everyone else. These vegan treats send a strong message that avoiding animal products does not condemn one to a dreary life of denial and deprivation.

For an analysis of nutrition, reputable organizations such as the American Dietetic Association,[1] American Cancer Society,[2] and American Heart Association[3] can be good sources. These organizations take hundreds, even thousands, of peer-reviewed studies, compiled over decades, and come to collective conclusions based on this research. Not surprisingly, they have all come to pretty much the same conclusions with reference to nutritional recommendations. Unfortunately, they lack the marketing power that food and supplement industries enjoy to get this message out to the public.

Simply put, every mainstream health organization recommends eating more vegetables, fruits, and whole grains and imposes restrictions on animal-product consumption.[4, 5, 6, 7] Eating a plant-based diet is universally recommended by all of these organizations, and vegetarianism and veganism are simply the natural extension of this recommendation. There is a reason mainstream health organizations are trying to get the public to eat more fruits, veggies, and whole grains. Plant-foods are high in disease-fighting fiber, phytochemicals,[8] and antioxidants; they have no artery-clogging cholesterol and are generally low in saturated fat (with the exception of coconuts, palm kernel oil, and an insignificant amount in nuts and seeds).[i] Conversely, animal products, whether they are local, free-range, sustainable, or from a backyard, have no fiber, phytochemicals, or significant amounts of antioxidants,[9] and they are loaded with cholesterol and saturated fat. They also bring a high risk factor for numerous chronic degenerative diseases like heart disease and stroke. The American Dietetic Association states,

> Appropriately planned vegetarian diets, including total vegetarian or vegan diets, are healthful, nutritionally adequate, and may provide health benefits in the prevention and treatment of certain diseases. Well-planned vegetarian diets are appropriate for individuals during all stages of the life cycle, including pregnancy, lactation, infancy, childhood, and adolescence, as well as for athletes.[10]

A hopeful sign that mainstream nutrition is moving in the veggie direction is the new food guide, *MyPlate*.[11] Recently unveiled by the United States Department of Agriculture (USDA), this new dietary guideline replaces the food pyramid that helped moms create healthy menus for the last two decades. The new guide takes plant-based eating even farther. MyPlate is an image of a dinner plate separated into four segments, with *grains* and *vegetables* making up the largest parts and *fruits* and *proteins* comprising the smaller sections. Not only is it very exciting that

---

i Another important piece of the healthy plant-based puzzle is to get a reliable source of Vitamin B12. Plant foods have some B12 but not consistently enough to be a reliable source of the vitamin. B12 is produced from bacteria, and in our sterile modern society, where we incessantly wash our food and drink purified water, B12 does not occur dependably in the vegan diet. However, it's easy for vegans to get their daily requirement of B12 from fortified foods like nondairy milks, fortified cereals, or supplements.

the vegetable and grain section take up by far the largest portions of the plate, indicating that one should eat these foods in greater quantity, but it is also noteworthy that vegetables, fruits, and grains are listed as food, while the fourth section, *protein*, is listed simply as a nutrient. It is not called *meat*, nor *meat/beans*; it is simply called *protein*. The other sections could be listed as *carbohydrates* or *vitamins*, but they are not. It is apparent that the USDA is specifically recommending eating vegetables, grains, and fruits; however, they consider how you get your protein to be optional. The clear message is that the US government no longer considers meat a required, or even recommended, part of a healthy diet. MyPlate signifies a turning point in mainstream nutrition education. This is practically a vegan plate.

Need another awesome reason—other than saving animals' lives and protecting the planet—to eat more plant foods? Researchers have found that vegetarians live significantly longer than meat-eaters. Male meat eaters live an average of 73.8 years, while vegetarian males live almost *ten years longer* at an average of 83.3 years. Non-vegetarian woman live an average of 79.6 years, while vegetarian women live a little over *six years longer* to an average of 85.7 years. The study, which looked at the diets of ninety-six thousand people, also found that vegetarians were typically thirty pounds lighter than meat eaters and had a considerably lower risk of diabetes.[12]

By contrast, there was a recent thirty-five-year follow-up to the Nurses' Health Study conducted by Harvard, one of the most extensive studies on the connection between diet and disease. It examined the leading risk factors for death and found that cholesterol was the greatest hazard in the United States, resulting in the number-one cause of death—heart disease. They discovered that consuming just one egg a day cut a woman's life as short as if she'd smoked five cigarettes a day for fifteen years.[13]

Cancer is the second-leading cause of death in the United States, and researchers are finding a strong dietary connection in at least 30 percent of all cancers. A study in 2012 of almost seventy thousand people—with a range of dietary styles including meat-eaters, semi-vegetarians, vegetarians who ate fish, vegetarian who ate dairy and eggs, and vegans—found that the greater the reduction of animal products in the diet, the greater the reduction of cancer risk. The report states, "Vegan diets showed statistically significant protection for overall cancer incidence in both genders combined and for female-specific cancers … compared to other dietary patterns."[14]

It looks like egg cartons should come with warning labels just as cigarettes do, because scientists are finding egg consumption is just as bad for you as smoking tobacco. Researchers measured the diet and smoking habits of participants and found a correlation between the number of egg yolks consumed and thickened artery walls, an indicator of heart health and probability of heart disease and heart attack. The association was nearly as high as the parallel between the amounts of tobacco smoked and thickened arteries.[15] The researchers concluded, "We believe our study makes it imperative to reassess the role of egg yolks, and dietary cholesterol in general, as a risk factor for coronary heart disease." Dietary cholesterol is only found in animal products.

Eggs are also linked to prostate cancer. A fourteen-year study observed the eating habits of twenty-seven thousand men and found that consuming just two and a half eggs per week made them 81 percent more likely to die from prostate cancer. Eating chickens was also a risk factor for poor prostate health.[16]

The animal consumption link to heart disease, stroke, and cancer are well established, but recent research also links meat-eating to lifelong asthma and hay fever. A study in the *Nutrition Journal* tracked the dietary habits of over 156,000 Australian men and women and found that the more meat they ate, the higher their risk of developing lifetime asthma and hay fever. The study's authors conclude, "Generally, diets marked by greater intakes of meats, poultry, and seafood were associated with diagnosed asthma and hay fever."[17]

Not only is there a strong concern that eating meat, dairy, and eggs puts you at higher risk for numerous chronic degenerative diseases,[18] there is also a danger from foodborne illness. Consumer Reports, an independent, nonprofit organization that provides product comparisons and ratings, tested whole broiler chickens for salmonella and campylobacter, the leading causes of foodborne disease, and found two-thirds of the carcasses tested positive for one or both of these dangerous bacteria. Of the organic chickens tested, 57 percent harbored campylobacter. [19] Dr. Michael Greger, a physician, author, and internationally recognized speaker on public-health issues, stated, "Campylobacter can trigger arthritis, heart and blood infections, and a condition called Guillain-Barré syndrome that can leave people permanently disabled and paralyzed. With the virtual elimination of polio, the most common cause of neuromuscular paralysis in the United States now comes from eating chicken."[20]

Contaminated fecal matter covering the remains of chickens is so prevalent that researchers at the University of Arizona found more fecal bacteria on kitchen sponges, dish towels, and in the sink drain of kitchens where meat is cooked than they found by swabbing toilets.[21] Dr. Greger concurs, "chicken 'juice' is essentially raw fecal soup."

Chicken isn't the only contaminated meat causing concern. Consumer Reports also found *Salmonella*, *Listeria*, *Staph* bacteria, and other antibiotic-resistant bacteria in much of the 240 samples of pork chops and ground pork tested. A full 69 percent of the samples contained *Yersinia*, a bacteria that can cause weeks of fevers, cramps, and bloody diarrhea. It is also associated with reactive arthritis and Crohn's disease, an inflammatory autoimmune condition of the gut. *Yersinia* infects one hundred thousand people annually in the United States alone—most are children.[22]

If heart disease and rampant bacteria weren't enough to worry about when looking at consumption of animal products, the Environmental Protection Agency (EPA) and the World Health Organization (WHO) warn of dietary dioxin in foods that originated from animals. Dioxin is an extremely toxic substance that can cause cancer or damage to the immune system, disrupt hormones, and cause developmental and reproductive problems in the womb. Dioxin is absorbed in fat tissue and can persist in the body for long periods of time. Bioaccumulation causes higher concentrations of dioxin up the food chain, hence the high levels present in animals. The WHO informs us that over 90 percent of human dioxin exposure is from meat, dairy, fish, and shellfish.[23]

Seafood is certainly not off the hook. Fish meat, like all animal meat, contains saturated fat, cholesterol, and a host of bacteria. Ninety-one percent of our seafood is imported, mostly from Asian fish farms, and it is rarely inspected by the FDA or the USDA. According to the Center for Disease Control and Prevention (CDC), seafood was responsible for more foodborne illness outbreaks than any other imported food between 2005 and 2010. Fish were responsible for 44 percent of sicknesses caused by imported food.[24] A recent study tested 330 samples of shrimp imported from the United States' number one supplier, Thailand. Sixty-seven percent tested positive for *Klebsiella*, a bacteria that can cause meningitis, pneumonia, and severe urinary-tract infections.[25] If that weren't disturbing enough, these strains were resistant to life-saving antibiotics—thirty-two strains showed resistance to eight different types of antibiotics. The study's researchers concluded that their "results indicate that imported shrimp is a reservoir for multidrug resistant *Klebsiella* and potential health risks posed by such strains should not be underestimated."[26]

This chapter is largely a synopsis on the benefits of plant-based nutrition versus animal product consumption. This cursory examination is in no way meant to be exhaustive, and we encourage further exploration of the abundant information on this subject. An excellent resource is the extensive work of Dr. Michael Greger. He has managed to present the most intricate details of the latest peer-reviewed nutrition information in a simple way that anyone can understand. His videos are usually just a couple of minutes in length; they are an incredibly informative and interesting way to get the best nutritional specifics available.[27] For further information, the work of T. Colin Campbell;[28] Dr. Neal Barnard;[29] and Jack Norris, RD[30] are worth exploring as well.

Exercise, adequate rest, and de-stressing techniques (whatever those are for you) are also important coauthors in your health story. Your well-being as a whole person is just as important as the care you wish to see bestowed on animals. With the large number of risk factors associated with consuming animal products, the stakes are high when eating steak. You are gambling with your health and your life. And when the benefits to the planet and the animals are taken into account, reducing or eliminating animal products is a venture well worth the minimal effort.

Chapter 11
Is Alternative Animal Production Healthy?

Nothing will benefit human health and increase the chances for survival of life on Earth as much as the evolution to a vegetarian diet.

—Albert Einstein

Consumer demand for new systems of raising animals is driven by the desire not only for improved animal welfare and for environmental benefits but also for a healthier product. We have learned in previous chapters that animal welfare in alternative animal production is only slightly better in some cases, yet the inevitable death of the animal negates any ethical benefit, and the touted environmental advantages can be a wash or worse than the conventional. But are these alternative techniques producing a product that promotes good health? People may believe that they are getting a healthier burger if the cow was grass-fed or an improved egg if the hen was cage-free, but the truth is more scrambled than straightforward.

Human contact with animals actually *creates* diseases, plagues, and pandemics—not just in modern animal agriculture but ever since we have been hunting, butchering, and domesticating animals. Nathan Wolfe a virologist, professor of epidemiology at University of California, Los Angeles (UCLA), and author of *The Viral Storm: The Dawn of a New Pandemic Age* has said, "Almost all of them (viruses) start from an animal virus, an animal microbe that jumps over to humans. That's actually the same with most of the major diseases of humanity. These things actually start with animals."[1]

One of our worst modern epidemics, which has killed millions since the first reported case thirty years ago, is HIV/AIDS. This deadly scourge's origins have now been traced back to the hunting, butchering, and eating of chimpanzees.[2] The chimps contracted the disease from their own violent actions of hunting other monkeys. The gruesomely intimate act of butchering an animal puts the hunter in contact with blood, entrails, bowels, and internal organs, and any viruses present need only to take a leisurely stroll over to the human host.[3]

More recently, a deadly form of avian flu, called the H5N1 strain, found its way to the human population via a young boy from a tiny village in northern Thailand. He was helping his grandfather on their small poultry farm, carrying sick birds from one area to another. He soon fell ill and was taken to a hospital, where he infected others and, unfortunately, died. Luckily this disease was not as contagious as the recent H1N1 swine flu virus that originated at an industrial pig operation in Mexico—it made an estimated sixty-one million people sick[4]—though the avian flu virus was much more lethal. According to Nathan Wolfe and other scientists, it is only a matter of time before a virus has the catastrophic combination of being both deadly and highly contagious, enabling it to kill millions almost as fast as we slaughter farmed animals.[5]

Animal diseases jump to humans and cause serious outbreaks not only in large-scale industrial farming but also in small-scale "local" farming in Africa, Asia, and other areas of rural concentration of people and animals. Most of the diseases that plague us are of our own making, due to close contact with sick animals. Many diseases are contracted from animals we eat, for example foot and mouth, avian flu, severe acute respiratory syndrome (SARS), bovine lung plague, swine fever (sometimes called hog cholera), mad cow disease, and Newcastle disease (a highly infectious disease originating in domestic poultry). Recently jumping from livestock to humans, a strain of the potentially deadly antibiotic-resistant bacterium known as methicillin-resistant *Staphylococcus aureus* (MRSA) has concerned researchers, who warn of a potential public health hazard.[6] The problem does not seem to be slowing, as 2011 saw zoonotic disease (infectious disease that is transmitted between species from animals to humans) outbreaks including foot and mouth disease in Paraguay, African swine fever in Russia, classic swine fever in Mexico, and bird flu in Asia. An article in *Science Daily* said, "A remarkable 61 percent of all human pathogens, and 75 percent of new human pathogens, are transmitted by animals, and some of the most lethal bugs affecting humans originate in our domesticated animals."[7] There is compelling evidence that measles, smallpox, influenza, diphtheria, the common cold, and tuberculosis may have all originated in other species and were originally transmitted to humans in the process of domestication and hunting.

New problems are arising with the recent trend in the United States and European countries toward giving animals more space and allowing them access to the outside. Animals free-roaming in pasture, or just having access to an outside area, are more susceptible to bacterial, viral, and parasitic infections as well as environmental contaminants.[8, 9, 10] Cases of *Toxoplasma gondii*, a dangerous parasitic disease, have plummeted in the last twenty years to the point of being practically nonexistent, but scientists are finding an alarming comeback in organically raised pigs.[11] A study in the *Journal of Food Protection* found that pigs with access to the outdoors had an increase in *T. gondii* infections.[12] *T. gondii* is particularly dangerous to pregnant woman and eating infected pork can cause spontaneous abortion and congenital disease.[13] The study also found that eggs from free-range hens had higher levels of dioxin. Dioxins are released into the environment though combustion and are considered highly toxic. They are believed to cause reproductive and developmental problems, damage the immune system, interfere with hormones, and also cause cancer.[14]

Another study compared pork loin samples from conventional and organic pig farming systems and found significantly higher *E. coli* contamination in the organic pork.[15] Taking a deeper look into the alternative-pork industry, Dr. Peter Davies wrote an extensive paper in the February 2011 issue of *Foodborne Pathogens and Disease* after finding that pigs with access to the outside were at a higher risk for numerous foodborne illnesses. Davies said, "Pigs raised in outdoor systems inherently confront higher risks of exposure to foodborne parasites."[16] It is a great irony that concerned people are seeking out these alternative labels partly—or solely—because they think it means a safer product. Yet animals exposed to the outdoors are at a greater risk of contracting numerous diseases, viruses, and parasites.

Among the numerous pathogens found to be on the rise in free-range farming of pigs is a nematode parasite called *Trichinella spiralis.* Like many of these diseases, *Trichinella spiralis* was quite deadly in the nineteenth century, and pork was a primary cause of infection. With the augment of industrial-farming techniques such as indoor confinement and rodent control, cases of this harmful parasite plummeted, with infections in modern times down 95 percent since the 1940s. However, if the trend toward free-ranging pigs continues, so will the increase in cases of this potentially fatal disease. Davies laments that if we continue down this path there will be "an eighty-fold greater risk (per pig produced) of *Trichinella* infections resulting from eating niche-market versus commercial pork products."[17]

The study also links an increase risk of *Toxoplasma gondii* and *Salmonella* to smaller animal group size. In other words, the smaller the farm operation, the higher the risk of these illnesses. *Taenia solium* is also on the rise in smaller operations. *T. solium* is a deadly parasite worldwide, because it thrives where there is poor sanitation. Foraging and free-ranging pigs are more susceptible to this bug that is practically nonexistent currently in the United States. But again, it could make a lethal comeback if free-ranging of animals comes more prominently into vogue.[18, 19]

Egg laying chickens are also at greater risk of bacterial and parasitic diseases when taken out of the conventional barren battery cages and allowed a colony caging or cage-free environment. They are also at risk of fowl cholera[20] and environmental contaminates such as arsenic, lead, and mercury, and selected persistent organochlorine compounds, dioxins, and dioxin-like polychlorinated biphenyls, dichlorodiphenyltrichloroethane (DDT), as well as other chlorinated pesticides.[21, 22] Colony cages are larger cages with enrichments such as nesting areas, dust-bathing litter, and perches. While colony cages are better than battery cages for the welfare of the birds, *E. coli* and other diseases abound when these production methods are used. *E. coli* is a bacterium that can cause severe stomach cramps, high fever, diarrhea, nausea, vomiting and, in extreme cases, death in humans. In one study, *E. coli* was the most common cause of death among 73 percent of litter-based (cage-free and colony cage) flocks and 74 percent of free-range (having access to the outside) flocks, compared with 65 percent in barren battery-caged flocks. Also amplified were injuries and deaths from increased pecking and mite infections.[23] Another study concluded that a consumer cannot assume that *Salmonella* risk will decrease in free-range and certified-organic chicken.[24]

While we feel strongly that chickens should have the space to live a seemingly more natural existence in colony caging, cage-free, and free-range systems, and we support efforts to move the industry in that direction, in some cases these techniques are increasing the likelihood of disease. The best solution for humans and chickens is to forego eating eggs altogether.

The new hobby of keeping backyard animals for their eggs and meat has hidden health hazards as well. In the summer of 2011, chicks from a mail order hatchery caused a multi-state *Salmonella* outbreak that sickened dozens of people in the fifteen states that ordered chicks by mail for backyard operations. The average age of the victims was four years old.[25] *The New England Journal of Medicine* had this to say regarding improvements at the hatcheries after the outbreak: "Interventions performed at the hatchery reduced, but did not eliminate, associated human infections, demonstrating the difficulty of eliminating *Salmonella* transmission from live poultry."[26] A chicken can appear perfectly healthy and be infected with *Salmonella*; she can then lay eggs that are infected as well.[27] Uneducated handlers can put their families at greater risk from contamination—when their intent was to have a safer experience.

Salmonella grows in the intestinal tract of an animal and is excreted in feces. Food that comes in direct or indirect contact with contaminated animal feces can infect humans when they eat it. Within twelve to seventy-two hours of eating an egg contaminated with *Salmonella*, a person can experience bloody diarrhea, fever, and/or severe abdominal cramps. The illness can last four to seven days, and if the symptoms are serious, hospitalization and antibiotics may be necessary. If the infection spreads from the intestines to the bloodstream, death is possible. Infants, the elderly, and people with compromised immune systems are at much greater risk.[28]

In the book *The Future of Organic Meats*, the authors state, "Consumers often perceive that organic meats are safer than conventional meats, but there is virtually no data to support this. This is partially due to the fact that the research results generated from studies published thus far are often inconsistent."[29] To be labeled organic, the animal products will be free of antibiotics, added hormones, and genetically altered materials, and they will have lower pesticide content—but studies show that there is no difference nutritionally between organic and conventional animal products. A Stanford mega-analysis of scores of existing studies compared conventional and organic produce, meat, and milk and found no significant difference in vitamins, minerals, protein, or fat content.[30]

We are in no way advocating keeping animals in cages or confinement sheds. On the contrary, we want to see animals roaming freely, expressing natural behaviors, and enjoying the simple pleasures of life—*on a sanctuary* where they will never be exploited for their bodies or killed for their meat. The intention in revealing that cage-free and free-ranging animals come with a new host of health concerns is to emphasize the point that raising animals for profit, no matter how it is done, will never be healthy for us, for the animals, or for the planet.

The basic composition of meat, milk, or egg, whether from a conventional or alternative source, is virtually unchanged, no matter how the animal was raised. They consist mainly of saturated fat and cholesterol, and they contain negligible amounts of cancer-fighting antioxidants and no fiber or phytochemicals, which are abundant in plant foods and essential to good health. Don't be fooled into thinking that just because an animal product is from an alternative source, all the health problems associated with animal products described in chapter 10 are negated. A piece of meat, no matter how the animal was raised, is still a piece of artery-clogging meat. An egg, no matter what the production method, is still a cholesterol and saturated fat-filled egg. Animal products, alternative or not, are still a high risk factor for disease. A plant-based diet rich in whole grains, legumes, vegetables, and fruits will offer more optimal health for everyone.

Chapter 12
Signs of Hope

It's pretty amazing to wake up every morning, knowing that every decision I make is to cause as little harm as possible. It's a fantastic way to live.

—Colleen Patrick-Goudreau,
Compassionate Cooks

The world has seen fast-paced progress for animal welfare in the last twenty or so years. With the scope of the animal protection movement growing and expanding, an evolution in the public's positive attitudes toward animals is blossoming. It is easier than ever to live a cruelty-free lifestyle. Plant-based food is abundant, and healthy food selections are appearing in mainstream groceries: bean and grain-based meats, plant-based cheeses, and a plethora of vegetables, legumes, whole grains, and fruit are easily found at any supermarket. Natural-food stores have the widest selection, with plant-based milks, nut cheeses, vegan pizza, and much more.

According to the *Wall Street Journal*, the number of products that were labeled meat-free or meatless grew 21 percent from 2009 to 2011. A new Harris Interactive study,[1] commissioned by the

Vegetarian Resource Group, found that the number of vegans in the United States has doubled since 2009 to 2.5 percent of the population. As of 2011, an amazing 7.5 million US citizens are following exclusively vegan diets that do not include any animal products—no meat, poultry, fish, dairy, or eggs. Close to sixteen million, or 5 percent, identify as vegetarian; they never eat meat, poultry, or fish. If this rate continues, vegans will account for 10 percent of the US population in 2015, 40 percent in 2019, and 80 percent in 2050! This would mean an end to the exploitation and suffering of billions of farmed animals. The study also revealed that 33 percent of US citizens are eating vegetarian meals a significant amount of the time and ordering vegetarian meals at restaurants. Though they are not vegetarian, these *flexetarians* number over one hundred million people—one third of the country—and are making a significant contribution to plummeting rates of meat consumption in the United States.

Interestingly, the demographic breakdown of the study discovered that there are equal percentages of both Democrats and Republicans eating vegetarian. Perhaps these two parties can agree on something—that plant-based eating is healthy and compassionate. This also illustrates that people avoiding meat are not your stereotypical hippie health nuts any longer. They are your neighbors and your coworkers, the store clerk and the little league coach, the dental hygienist and the babysitter. There is no "type" anymore, as our numbers exceed the tens of millions and continue to quickly rise.

A survey by Bon Appétit Management Company, which manages numerous corporate, college, and university dining services nationwide, found that the number of college students eating plant-based diets has dramatically increased in just a few years. Among college students, this survey[2] found that 12 percent are vegetarian and 2 percent are vegan. In just four years, vegetarian diets rose by 50 percent and vegan diets had doubled between their 2005–2006 poll and their 2009–2010 poll.[3] These young people are the future of our country, and they are quickly becoming compassionate and ecologically aware eaters.

Egg consumption has dramatically decreased in recent years, according to the United Egg Producers. Based on statistics from the United States Department of Agriculture, the typical US citizen ate an average of 258.1 eggs in 2006. Just five years later, in 2011, consumption had dropped down to 246.3, nearly one dozen fewer eggs per person.[4] Perhaps this indicates that people are seeing the rotten truth behind egg production and recognizing that hens suffer terribly to produce eggs for human consumption.

The number of animals killed for food in the United States has dropped as well. Due to an oversupply brought on by low demand, chicken slaughter slowed dramatically in the second half of 2011. According to a United States Department of Agriculture report, third-quarter production is estimated to be 1.3 percent lower than the third quarter of 2010. Lower production is expected to continue in the fourth quarter of 2011, with production expected to decrease 2 percent from the same period in 2010.[5]

A study from the *Daily Livestock Report* [6] found that US meat, poultry, and fish consumption declined by one pound per person in 2010. Per capita pork consumption fell by 2.2 pounds per person in 2010, and beef consumption was at its lowest level in 2010 since the *Daily Livestock Report* started keeping records in 1955. This is the fourth year in a row that meat consumption has declined in the United States and the fifth decline within a six-year period. Studies are finding that a recent increased awareness about farmed animal suffering is likely to be a contributing factor to the decline.

In the last decade there has also been a radical shift in the halls of government, and thanks to powerful animal protection groups like the Humane Society of the United States (HSUS), legislators are starting to pay attention to issues regarding farmed-animal treatment. For the first time, laws are being passed to protect animals in the farming sector and relieve their immense suffering. In 2002, there were virtually no laws on the books for the protection of farmed animals. In the last ten years, nine states have passed laws to prohibit cruel practices such as confining pigs, calves, and chickens in tiny cages, cutting off dairy cows' tails, and force-feeding ducks for foie gras. Customer concern is driving major retailers to demand improved treatment of animals from their suppliers. This is a huge boon for the animal-protection movement, as the history of most social, political, and civil rights struggles shows that they can become increasingly effective as laws begin to protect the oppressed. Not only do these animal-protection laws make the lives of animals in industrial agriculture a little less horrible, they educate the public about the truth of modern farming and awaken people to the plight of the animals they eat. Public opinion shifts in favor of the exploited and subjugated when our legislature steps in to guard them from unfair treatment and harm. Support for these reforms is crucial to the rapid success of total abolition for animals.

Vegan Celebrities and Athletes

Conscientious eating is going mainstream. There are more celebrities, politicians, and athletes than ever before who are leaving animals off their plates. Bill Clinton, Ellen DeGeneres, Anne Hathaway, Lea Michele, Natalie Portman, Woody Harrelson, and Joaquin Phoenix are just a few of the famous vegans in the spotlight. Being vegan is no longer synonymous with being weak or skinny. Vegan athletes and bodybuilders are breaking stereotypes, building muscle, and winning competitions—all using plant power!

Scott Jurek, age thirty-seven, is an ultramarathoner. What make a marathon *ultra*? Well, the races he has been winning make a regular marathon of just over 26 miles look like an easy jog on the elliptical machine. Jurek has not only run in but twice *won* the 153-mile Badwater Ultramarathon in Death Valley, and he has won the 100-mile Western States Endurance Run a staggering seven times. He once ran 165.7 miles in one day, making him the US record holder for a twenty-four-hour run. Oh, and by the way, he's vegan.

Jurek has been running races since 1994. He went vegan in 1999, and that's when he started to win. He cites his vegan diet as the reason for his incredible health and recovery in training. Jurek feels that it is important as an athlete and an environmentalist that he take his diet all the way to vegan.[7] Even the American Dietetic Association encourages athletes to increase their vegetable and fruit intake, and they readily admit that no animal protein is required to build muscle.[8]

Ricardo Moreira doesn't worry about not getting enough protein. This vegan cage fighter is solid as steel, but has a heart of gold. The lifelong martial artist says that he has always loved animals. Moreira says, "Within the martial arts, there are many codes of conduct, one of which is to respect all forms of life. Veganism goes hand in hand with my martial arts training and philosophy."

Vegan bodybuilders are breaking the mold. Robert Cheeke, Kenneth Williams, Chad Byers, and others are winning championships and triumphing over other athletes, who see these pumped-up, hard bodies and want to know their secret. Their secret is a plant-based diet. It seems you can no longer typecast vegans as undernourished and gaunt. Celebrities, athletes, and healthy vegans everywhere are showing the world how vigorous, energetic, and dynamic vegans can be.[9]

Veganic Farming

Here's a label to look for in the future: *veganic*. Many in modern agriculture will argue that you can't grow plants without animal inputs, in the form of fertilizers like manure and bone meal. Well, tell that to a veganic farmer and he will set you straight, with a sweet strawberry grown without anything that came from an animal. Veganic, or vegan-organic gardening insures that the plants and soil are not only pesticide and herbicide-free but that nothing from an animal is ever used in the production. Gaining in popularity in Canada, the United States, and in the United Kingdom, this method of growing produce is sometimes referred to as "stock-free farming."

Conventional modern agriculture uses a variety of animal inputs, such as livestock feces, blood and bone meal, slaughterhouse sludge, and fish emulsion to grow vegetables and grains. Using these products not only supports industries that exploit animals but also exposes us to substances that are unhealthy and unsafe (think *E. coli*). When there's a recall of a plant food for bacterial contamination, like spinach, for instance, it can usually be traced back to animal feces in the field. All too often Bessie is to blame, not Popeye. Although these animal by-products are not the primary profitable product for the animal industry, selling them can offset costs and make the company more profitable. Veganic produce offers a cruelty-free option that does not give money to the industry of animal exploitation.

As you walk the dirt path to visit the animals at Animal Place, you pass an abundant garden with rows of a variety of greens, vegetables, and fruits soaking up the Grass Valley, California sun. Greg Litus maintains the facilities for Animal Place and also monitors the pasture and water quality for the farm. When he is not supervising the fields, he is busy tending the three-acre veganic garden that feeds the staff, interns, and volunteers, as well as selling produce to visitors. "We wanted to show that it can be done, and done well," Greg said. He and his wife, farm manager Stephanie Litus, have labored with dirt on their hands— but no blood—to grow vegetables, with respect for animals and the environment foremost in mind. Greg says, "This farm is an important tool in the process of building a cruelty-free world."

How do they do it? Veganic farming requires a combination of vegetable compost, crop rotation, mulching, and other sustainable, ecologically sound methods. Fertilizers that are veganic and ecologically friendly include hay mulch, wood ash, composted organic matter (fruit/vegetable peels, leaves, and grass clippings), green manures and nitrogen-fixing cover crops (fava beans, clover, alfalfa), and seaweed (fresh, liquid, or meal) for trace elements. There is even a veganic certification offered though the Veganic Agriculture Network.[10] As with organic certification, three years of compliance is required for the official label Veganic. This progressive method of growing food is not widely available, but there are farms in some areas selling at farmers' markets and offering boxes on their CSA (Community Supported Agriculture) farms. More are sprouting up all the time.

Exposure of abusive animal agriculture, legislation being passed to protect animals, meat consumption and production on a downward spiral, Hollywood going vegan—these are all shards in a mosaic of rising awareness. An inevitable snowball effect is developing as history quickly rolls us in the direction of kindness for all the world's creatures. Don't you want to be on the compassionate side of history?

Conclusion

After all the research, reading, field work, and interviews we conducted for this book, we are now convinced that the state of alternative animal agriculture is actually worse than we thought when we started this project. We found time and again that the conditions for the animals are only marginally improved by alternative farming methods and inherent cruelties still abound. The environmental improvements are negligible at best, and if this trend grows, we will be using and abusing more and more land and water. There is just not enough space to pasture-raise millions of animals in any sort of free-roaming operations. Dramatic reductions of greenhouse gas emissions are needed fast, and one of our best hopes to achieve this, scientists agree, is a global transition to a plant-based diet. *It is not our methods of animal agricultural practices that need to change; it is our unwillingness to let go of animal products and animal farming.*

Just because a farm is small does not mean it is exempt from cruelty. Just because an animal product is labeled alternative does not mean that it was inspected to be held accountable for compliance. Just because a company depicts peaceful pastures on their website does not mean that all is well on that farm. Just because a business puts a pleasant picture on their carton does not mean that those in their care are happy animals producing happy meat, milk, and eggs. It is quite the contrary. There is an intrinsic element of cruelty in animal agriculture that cannot be eliminated with any small-scale operation or organic label. Animal agriculture is a business that makes money on the bodies of other sentient beings. This can never be free of a fundamental insensitivity toward animals, the subjects of the industry's profits. It is a deep betrayal to the animals that depend on humans for care. In the same way that one cannot own humans and traffic their bodies for profit in a humane way, it is impossible to humanely profit from the lives and bodies of animals.

Consumers hold the power, and once they learn the truth—that they are being deceived into paying higher prices for products that are unhealthy and do not to live up to the environmental and animal welfare standard that they were touted to—then they will take their compassion elsewhere and stop supporting animal agriculture altogether. By transitioning to a plant-based diet, they will make the most healthful choice for the planet, the animals, and their families. They will do this because they care. A simple reduction in the amount of animal products a family eats weekly can lead to vast improvements in the state of our world. The more we reduce our consumption of animal products, the better life will be for animals, the planet, and our own health.

Shortly after you put down this book, you will be eating. Now that you are equipped with a full pantry of information regarding issues involving food production, we hope that you will approach that meal, and all meals to come, with consciousness, awareness, and honesty. If you didn't already, you now realize the capability that food has to nourish or damage our bodies, to help or harm animals, to protect or destroy the planet. As humans, we have a unique opportunity—a rare gift. We can actually control and stop the suffering and killing of other species, particularly farmed animals. We have that power. A coyote can't control his instinct to kill for food; a lion can't restrain his need to hunt for sustenance. For them, eating involves neither morality nor ethics; it simply stems from necessity. But *we can* make the conscious choice to not kill animals for our food, and we can actually be healthier as a result. It is a beautiful gift that we can give the world to ease suffering, stop the killing of billions of animals, drastically reduce global warming, and lower rates of obesity and chronic degenerative diseases. With the abundance of plant-based options and a little bit of commitment and integrity, it's easy. Why would we not do this for a more peaceful, compassionate future? It is our obligation as thinking, rational, supposedly superior beings to make this powerful and simple choice to live a cruelty-free life. Let's create a compasionate, healthy, and thriving world together.

> *You may choose to look the other way but you can never say again that you did not know.*

> —William Wilberforce

Resources

Videos

Auction Yard Videos
www.mercyforanimals.org/auction/video.aspx
www.cok.net/camp/inv/auction/videos.php

Hatchery Videos

www.cok.net/camp/inv/calcruz09
www.cok.net/camp/inv/turkeys06

Veal Calf Investigation

www.humanesociety.org/news/news/2009/10/calf_
investigation_103009.html

Pork Production Video

www.mercyforanimals.org/pigs

Fish Production Video

www.mercyforanimals.org/fish

Farm Animal Sanctuaries

Farm Sanctuary: www.farmsactuary.org
Animal Place: www.animalplace.org

Websites/Blogs

Compassion Over Killing: www.cok.net
Mercy for Animals: www.mercyforanimals.org
A Well-Fed World: www.awellfedworld.org
United Poultry Concerns: www.upc-online.org
Animal Legal Defense Fund: www.aldf.org
Carnism Awareness and Action Network (CAAN): www.carnism.com
Michael Greger, MD: www.drgreger.org
Eating Plants Blog, James McWilliams: www.james-mcwilliams.com
Our Hen House: www.ourhenhouse.org
Free From Harm: www.freefromharm.org

Books

Why We Love Dogs, Eat Pigs and Wear Cows, by Dr. Melanie Joy

The 30-Day Vegan Challenge and *The Vegan's Daily Companion*, by Colleen Patrick-Goudreau

The Pig Who Sang to the Moon: The Emotional World of Farm Animals, by Jeffrey Moussaieff Masson

Comfortably Unaware, by Dr. Richard Oppenlander

The World Peace Diet, by Dr. Will Tuttle

Change of Heart: What Psychology Can Teach Us about Spreading Social Change, by Nick Cooney

Striking at the Roots: A Practical Guide to Animal Activism, by Mark Hawthorne

Index

Symbols

Concentrated Animal Feeding Operations (CAFO) 117

A

agricultural exemption 34
air pollution 116, 117, 122
American Cancer Society 169
American Dietetic Association 169, 170, 188
American Heart Association 169
ammonia 41, 116, 117, 120, 121
anaerobic digestion 145
anesthesia 46, 58
Anhang, Jeff 111
Animal Legal Defense Fund 44, 66
Animal Place 18, 69, 91, 190
antioxidants 169, 183
aquaculture 150, 151
artificial insemination 25, 34, 36, 77
auction 36, 39, 77
Aurora Organic Dairy 84
avian flu 177, 178

B

backyard slaughter 79, 89, 99, 100

Barnard, Neal 175
battery cages 72, 73, 74, 85, 180
beef 36, 38, 70, 71, 77, 119, 131, 132
Bekoff, Marc xxii, 29
betrayal 5, 7, 14, 15, 99, 100, 107, 108
biodiversity 109, 111, 113, 120, 134
bluefin tuna 148
boar taint 57
bolt gun 25, 48, 49, 53
broiler chicken 41
Broom, Donald xxvii
by-catch/by-kill 147, 152

C

cage-free 40, 41, 58, 74, 75, 180, 181, 182
calf xxiii, 35, 36, 37, 51
Campbell, T. Colin 175
cancer 172, 173, 174, 179, 183
Capper, Jude 131
carbon dioxide (CO2) 112, 113, 115, 122, 149
castration 46, 57, 58, 85, 86
catch and release 157, 158
catfish 157

vegetarian 119, 170, 171, 172, 176,
185, 186
visceral veganism 27

W

waste lagoons 114, 120
water pollution 120, 121
water wasted 117, 118, 119, 131
Watson, Paul 146, 159
Whole Foods 42, 43, 76, 153
Wolfe, Nathan 177
World Health Organization 174
world hunger 124
World Preservation Foundation 113,
212

Z

zoonotic disease 178

Notes

Introduction

1. "Rural poll finds concern about animal welfare, doubt about new regulations," *High Plains/Midwest Ag Journal.*

2. "Consumer Support for Animal Welfare", Global Animal Partnership, 2013, http://www.globalanimalpartnership.org/for-retailers/consumer-support-for-animal-welfare/

3. A. Bufalari, et al., "Pain assessment in animals." Veterinary Research Communications, August 2007, pp. 55-58

4. V. Molony and J. E. Kent, "Assessment of acute pain in farm animals using behavioral and physiological measurements." Journal of Animal Science, January 1997

5. Daniel M. Weary et al., "Identifying and preventing pain in animals" Animal Welfare Program, Faculty of Land and Food Systems, University of British Columbia, October 2006

6. A. U. Butterworth, J. A. Mench, and N. Wielebnowski, "Practical strategies to assess (and improve) welfare" Division of Food Animal Science, Bristol, UK: University of Bristol, Langford House, 2011

7. Mellor, D. J., and K. J. Stafford, "Integrating practical, regulatory and ethical strategies for enhancing farm animal welfare" Australian Veterinary Journal, Vol. 79, no 11, 762–768, 2001

8. J. C. Swanson, "Farm animal well-being and intensive production systems," Journal of Animal Science 73. No 9, September 1995

9. Guatteo, R. et al., "Minimizing pain in farm animals: the 3S approach – 'Suppress, Substitute, Soothe'" Cambridge University Press, August 2012

10. Lara Désiré, Alain Boissy, and Isabelle Veissier, "Emotions in farm animals: a new approach to animal welfare in applied ethology," Behavioural Processes 60, no 2 , Pages 165–180, November–December 2002

11. R. Dantzer, "Can farm animal welfare be understood without taking into account the issues of emotion and cognition?" Integrative Neurobiology, Journal of Animal Sciences, 2002

12. Francis Crick Memorial Conference, http://fcmconference.org/

13. Philip Low et al, "The Cambridge Declaration of Consciousness" Francis Crick Memorial Conference on Consciousness in Human and non Human Animals, July 7, 2012

14. Bekoff, Marc. 2011. Dead Cow Walking, The Case Against Born-Again Carnivorism. *The Atlantic.*

15. "Cows suffer stress when separated from their best friends": BioNews Bioscholar, July 5, 2011, http://news.bioscholar.com/2011/07/cows-suffer-stress-when-separated-from-their-best-friends.html.

16. L. Rogers, "The Development of Brain and Behaviour in the Chicken." Oxfordshire, UK: CABI Publishing, 1995

17. S. M. Abeyesinghe, C. J. Nicol, S. J. Hartnell, and C.M. Wathes, "Can domestic fowl, *Gallus gallus domesticus*, show self-control?" Animal Behavior 70, July 2005

18. J. L. Edgar, J. C. Lowe, E.S. Paul, and C. J. Nicol, "Avian Maternal Response to Chick Distress," Proceedings of the Royal Society Biological Sciences, February 14, 2011

19. "Study Shows Hens Empathize With Other Birds," The Poultry Site news, March 16, 2011, http://www.thepoultrysite.com/poultrynews/22214/study-shows-hens-empathise-with-other-birds

20. Kendrick, K. M., "Sheep Senses, Social Cognition and Capacity for Consciousness" The Welfare of Sheep; Animal Welfare, 2008.

21. C. Lee, S. Colegate, and A. Fisher, "Development of a maze test and its application to assess spatial learning and memory in Merino sheep" Applied Animal Behaviour Science 96, no 1, pp. 43–51, January 2006

22. A. Jennifer Morton and Laura Avanzo, "Executive Decision-Making in the Domestic Sheep" Public Library of Science, 2011

23. "Crafty sheep conquer cattle grids" BBC News, July 30, 2004, http://news.bbc.co.uk/2/hi/uk_news/3938591.stm.

24. Helft, Miguel. 1997, "Pig Video Arcades Critique Life in the Pen," Wired Magazine

25. Donald Broom, "Pigs learn what a mirror image represents and use it to obtain information," Animal Behavior 78, no 5, November 2009

Chapter 1

1. Dictionary.com, "humane" http://dictionary.reference.com/browse/humane

2. "Facts About the Death Penalty," Death Penalty Information Center, Sept. 26, 2012, Deathpenaltyinfo.org

3. Grillo, Robert. "Defending Animals from Cultural Bias and Journalistic Integrity" Free From Harm Blog, 2013

4. Joy, Melanie. *Why We Love Dogs, Eat Pigs and Wear Cows,* Conari Press, 2010, pp. 29–30

5. S. Rachman, Adam S. Radomsky, Corinna M. Elliott, Eva Zysk, "Mental Contamination: The Perpetrator Effect" Department of Psychology, University of British Columbia, Vancouver, pp. 587–593, August 2010 The authors define the "perpetrator effect" thus: when subjects committed nonconsensual scenarios that involved a violation of ethical norms, they would experience a substantial increase in negative emotions, "notably shame, disgust, and guilt."

6. M. S. Kim, A. M. Lefcourt, and Y. R. Chen, "Optimal Fluorescence Excitation and Emission Bands for Detection of Fecal Contamination," Journal of Food Protection 66, no. 7, July 2003

7. B. Cho, M. S. Kim, K. Chao, K. Lawrence, B. Park, and K. Kim, "Detection of fecal residue on poultry carcasses by laser-induced fluorescence imaging," Journal of Food Science 74, no 3, 2009

8. A. Sharif and G. Muhammad, "Somatic cell count as an indicator of udder heath status under modern dairy production: A review" Livestock and Dairy Development Department, Punjab, Lahore; University of Agriculture, Faisalabad, Pakistan, 2008

9. From Old English *mete* "food" or "article of food," of Germanic origin.

Chapter 2

1. Dr. M. L. O'Connor, "Artificial Insemination Technique" Dairy Integrated Reproductive Management, Pennsylvania State University

2. confirmed in a conversation with a Clover Dairy lab worker, October 2, 2012

3. Ibid

4. P. R. Wiepkema, K. K. Van Hellemond, P. Roessingh, and H. Romberg, "Behaviour and abomasal damage in individual veal calves," Applied Animal Behaviour Science, Pages 257–268, October 1997

5. Don P. Blayney, "The Changing Landscape of Milk Production," United States Department of Agriculture, June 2002

6. Kristof, Nicholas. "Where Cows Are Happy and Food is Healthy" *New York Times,* September 8, 2012

7. Cheng, Heng Wei, "Pain in Chickens and Effects of Beak Trimming," Agricultural Research Service, United States Department of Agriculture, April 2010

8. "An HSI Report: the welfare of animals in the egg industry" Humane Society International, Agriculture; Behavioral Sciences; Veterinary Sciences; March 2000

9. confirmed in a conversation with Kathy Nichols, owner of Chino Valley Ranch (Human Harvest eggs is one of their products), October 15, 2012.

10. "An HSI Report: the welfare of animals in the egg industry" Humane Society International, Agriculture; Behavioral Sciences; Veterinary Sciences; March 2000

11. Davis Karen PhD. "Remembering Turkeys at Thanksgiving" United Poultry Concerns, November 21, 2012 www.upc-online.org

12. "Shipping Fever Pneumonia," The Merck Veterinary Manual, Merck Sharp & Dohme Corp., a subsidiary of Merck & Co., Inc., Whitehouse Station, NJ, 2011

13. A. Pointon, A. Kiemeier, and N. Pointon, "Review of the impact of pre-slaughter feed curfews of cattle, sheep and goats on food safety and carcase hygiene in Australia," Food Control 26, no 2,) pp. 313–321, August 2012

14. Kathryn Gillespie, "How Happy is Your Meat?: Confronting (Dis) connectedness in the 'Alternative' Meat Industry," The Brock Review 12, no 1, p. 107, 2011

15. Davis, Karen, PhD. "Prisoned Chickens, Poisoned Eggs: An Inside Look at the Modern Poultry Industry" Book Publishing Company, Chapter 5, 2009

16. Sara Shields, PhD., Mohan Raj, Ph.D., "A Humane Society of the United States Report: The Welfare of Birds at Slaughter" The Humane Society of the United States, 2008

17. confirmed in conversation with "David," an undercover investigator

18. "Improvements for Poultry Slaughter Inspection" Appendix C – Literature Review of the Poultry Slaughter Process, US Department of Agriculture, Food and Safety Inspection Service

19. Sara Sara Shields, PhD., Mohan Raj, Ph.D., "A Humane Society of the United States Report: The Welfare of Birds at Slaughter" The Humane Society of the United States, 2008

20. Kathryn Gillespie, "How Happy is Your Meat?: Confronting (Dis)connectedness in the 'Alternative' Meat Industry," The Brock Review 12, no 1, p. 101, 2011

21. "Humane Methods of Livestock Slaughter" United States Code, Chapter 48, Washington DC: GPO, 2011

22. D. K. Blackmore, "Euthanasia; not always Eu," Australian Veterinary Journal 70, no 11, November 1993

23. Kathryn Gillespie, "How Happy is Your Meat?: Confronting (Dis)connectedness in the 'Alternative' Meat Industry," The Brock Review 12, no 1, p. 106-107, 2011

24. "Mobile Slaughter Unit Compliance Guide" Food Safety and Inspection Service, US Department of Agriculture

25. Kathryn Gillespie, "How Happy is Your Meat?: Confronting (Dis)connectedness in the 'Alternative' Meat Industry," The Brock Review 12, no 1, p. 109, 2011

26. "Mobile Slaughter" Unit Compliance Guide" Food Safety and Inspection Service, US Department of Agriculture

27. Berlin, Loren. "Beef we can believe in: Why sustainably farmed meat is good for us and the environment, *Ode Magazine*, July/August 2011.

28. Finz, Stacy. "Niman Ranch Founder Challenges New Owners," SF Gate, February 22, 2009

29. Hot Shot Power Mite Compact Livestock Prod sold at Jeffers Livestock, http://www.jefferspet.com

30. M. A. Sutherland, B. L. Davis, T. A. Brooks, and J. J. McGlone, "Physiology and behavior of pigs before and after castration: effects of two topical anesthetics," Animal : An International Journal of Animal Bioscience 4, no 12, December 2010

31. Martin Leidig, Barbara Hertrampf, Klaus Failing, Anslem Schumann, and Gerald Reiner, "Pain and discomfort in male piglets during surgical castration with and without local anesthesia as determined by vocalization

and defense behavior," Applied Animal Behaviour Science 116, no 2–4, January 31,2009

32. S. Wing, D. Cole, and G. Grant, "Environmental injustice in North Carolina's hog industry" National Institute of Environmental Health Science, March 2000

Chapter 3

1. "Farm Animal Welfare: An Assessment of Product Labeling Claims, Industry Quality Assurance Guidelines, and Third Party Certification Standards" A Farm Sanctuary Report, University of California

2. Jeannette Beranger, "How To Raise Heritage Turkeys on Pasture, Value-Added Considerations, Alternative Farming System and Labeling" American Livestock Breeds Conservancy; Global Resource Action Center for the Environment (GRACE) Sustainable Table Program, p. 91

3. "Meat and Poultry Labeling Terms" US Department of Agriculture Fact Sheet, April 12, 2011

4. "Laying Hen Housing," Animal Welfare, American Veterinary Medical Association

5. "Farm Animal Welfare: An Assessment of Product Labeling Claims, Industry Quality Assurance Guidelines, and Third Party Certification Standards" A Farm Sanctuary Report, University of California pp. 21–22

6. Jeannette Beranger, "How To Raise Heritage Turkeys on Pasture, Value-Added Considerations, Alternative Farming System and Labeling" American Livestock Breeds Conservancy; Global Resource Action Center for the Environment (GRACE) Sustainable Table Program, p. 89

7. "Free-Range and Other Meat and Poultry Terms, Free-Range or Free Roaming" Mayo Clinic Website, accessed September 24, 2012, http://www.mayoclinic.com/health/free-range/MY01559

8. "Farm Animal Welfare: An Assessment of Product Labeling Claims, Industry Quality Assurance Guidelines, and Third Party Certification Standards" A Farm Sanctuary Report, University of California pp. 24–25

9. Michael C. Appleby, "The European Union Ban on Conventional Cages for Laying Hens: History and Prospects," Journal of Applied Animal Welfare Science, Volume 6, Issue 2, 2003

10. "Farm Animal Welfare: An Assessment of Product Labeling Claims, Industry Quality Assurance Guidelines, and Third Party Certification Standards" A Farm Sanctuary Report, University of California p. 21

11. "Free-Range and Other Meat and Poultry Terms, Cage-Free" Mayo Clinic Website, accessed September 24, 2012, http://www.mayoclinic.com/health/free-range/MY01559

12. Clover Stornetta Farms website home page, http://cloverstornetta.com/

13. Confirmed in a phone conversation with Clover Dairy lab worker, October 2, 2012

14. McWilliams, James E. *Just Food: Where Locavores Get It Wrong and How We Can Truly Eat Responsibly*, Little, Brown & Co., 2009

15. "Farm Animal Welfare: An Assessment of Product Labeling Claims, Industry Quality Assurance Guidelines, and Third Party Certification Standards" A Farm Sanctuary Report, University of California p. 27

16. "Free-Range and Other Meat and Poultry Terms" Mayo Clinic Website, accessed September 24, 2012, http://www.mayoclinic.com/health/free-range/MY01559

17. Carolyn Dimitri and Lydia Oberholtzer, "Marketing US Organic Foods: Recent Trends From Farms to Consumers" USDA Economic Research Service, Economic Information Bulletin, September 2009

18. Marley, C L; Weller, R F; Neale, M; Main, D.C.J.; Roderick, S; Keatinge, R, "Aligning health and welfare principles and practice in organic dairy systems: a review," *Animal : an international journal of animal bioscience* 4. 2 (February 2010): 259–271.

19. "Health and Welfare in Organic Poultry Production" Swedish University Agricultural Science, Department, Animal, Environment & Health, Skara, Sweden, March 31, 2002

20. "Meat and Poultry Labeling Terms" US Department of Agriculture Fact Sheet, April 12. 2011, p. 7

21. Kathryn Gillespie, "How Happy is Your Meat?: Confronting (Dis) connectedness in the 'Alternative' Meat Industry," The Brock Review 12, no 1, p. 111, 2011

22. F. Napolitano, G. De Rosa, V. Ferrante, F. Grasso, and A. Braghieri, "Monitoring the welfare of sheep in organic and conventional farms using an ANI 35 L derived method" Small Ruminant Research 83, pp. 49–57, May 2009

23. P.B. Gade, "Welfare of animal production in intensive and organic systems with special reference to Danish organic pig production" Danish Meat Research Institute , 2002

24. A. Rosati and A. Aumaitre, "Organic dairy farming in Europe" Livestock Production Science 90, no 1, pp. 41–51. October 2004

25. A. J. Bradley, "Bovine Mastitis: An Evolving Disease" The Veterinary Journal 164, no 2, September 2002

26. "Farm Animal Welfare: An Assessment of Product Labeling Claims, Industry Quality Assurance Guidelines, and Third Party Certification Standards" A Farm Sanctuary Report, University of California

27. A Farm Sanctuary Report, p. 73, *ibid*

28. A Farm Sanctuary Report, *ibid*

Chapter 4

1. Sellers, Patricia. "Mark Zuckerberg's new challenge: Eating only what he kills (and yes, we do mean literally...)," CNN Money online, May 26, 2011

2. Elwood , Ian. "On the Chopping Block in Oakland," San Francisco Bay Guardian Online, May 24, 2011

3. Kathryn Gillespie, "How Happy is Your Meat?: Confronting (Dis) connectedness in the 'Alternative' Meat Industry," The Brock Review 12, no 1, p. 120, 2011

4. "Oakland Food System Assessment," Mayor's Office of Sustainability, Oakland, California

5. "HSUS Report: welfare issues with transport of day-old chicks," Humane Society of the United States, SC Agriculture; Veterinary Sciences , 2008

6. as sited by James McWilliams, "Killing What you Eat, The Dark Side of Compassionate Carnivores" September, 2011, www.freakonomics.com

7. as sited by James McWilliams, "Killing What you Eat, The Dark Side of Compassionate Carnivores" September, 2011, www.freakonomics.com

8. as sited by James McWilliams, "Killing What you Eat, The Dark Side of Compassionate Carnivores" September, 2011, www.freakonomics.com

Chapter 5

1. Pamela Martin and Gidon Eshel, "Diet, Energy and Global Warming," Department of Geophysical Sciences, University of Chicago, Dec 12, 2005

2. Schwartz, Peter, Randall, Doug, "An Abrupt Climate Change Scenario and its Implications for United States National Security," California Institute of Technology Jet Propulsion Lab, October, 2003

3. Doug Gurian-Sherman, "Raising the Steaks: Global Warming and Pasture Raised Beef Production in the United States," Union of Concerned Scientists, February 2011

4. "Top Name Brands Implicated in Amazon Destruction," Greenpeace website, June 1, 2009

5. H. Steinfeld et al, "Livestock's Long Shadow, Environmental Issues and Opinions," Food and Agriculture Organization of the United Nations, 2006

6. H. Steinfeld et al, "Livestock's Long Shadow, Environmental Issues and Opinions," Food and Agriculture Organization of the United Nations, 2006

7. Edgar G. Hertwich, "Assessing the Environmental Impacts of Consumption and Production: Priority Products and Materials," United Nations International Panel for Sustainable Resource Management, June 2010

8. Christopher Field, Vincente Barros, Thomas Stocker, Qin Dhae, "Managing the Risks of Extreme Events and Disasters To Advance Climate Change Adaptation," Special Report of the Intergovernmental Panel on Climate Change Cambridge University Press, 2012,

9. "Weather Extremes In a Changing Climate: Hindsight on Foresight," World Meteorological Organization, 2011

10. Robert Goodland and Jeff Anhang, "Livestock and Climate Change," *World Watch*, Nov./December 2009

11. H. Steinfeld et al, "Livestock's Long Shadow, Environmental Issues and Opinions," Food and Agriculture Organization of the United Nations, 2006, p.22

12. H. Steinfeld et al, "Livestock's Long Shadow, Environmental Issues and Opinions," Food and Agriculture Organization of the United Nations, 2006, p.26

13. Pamela Martin and Gidon Eshel, "Diet, Energy and Global Warming," Department of Geophysical Sciences, University of Chicago, Dec 12, 2005

14. H. Steinfeld et al, "Livestock's Long Shadow, Environmental Issues and Opinions," Food and Agriculture Organization of the United Nations, 2006

15. "Reducing Shorter-Lived Climate Forcers through Dietary Change," World Preservation Foundation, p. 3

16. "Reducing Shorter-Lived Climate Forcers through Dietary Change," World Preservation Foundation

17. "Soy Granule- How Sustainable is it Really?," Sustainable Europe Research Institute, Sept. 2, 2012

18. Roller, "Energy Costs of Intensive Livestock Production," *Diet for a New America* cited, American Society of Agriculture Engineers

19. Pamela Martin and Gidon Eshel, "Diet, Energy and Global Warming," Department of Geophysical Sciences, University of Chicago, Dec 12, 2005

20. "Hazards, Pollution from Factory Farms: An Analysis of the EA's Air Emissions Monitoring Study Data" Environmental Integrity Project, March 2011

21. "Hazards, Pollution from Factory Farms: An Analysis of the EA's Air Emissions Monitoring Study Data" Environmental Integrity Project, p. 2, March 2011

22. "Sustainability of Meat-Based and Plant-Based Diets and the Environment" American Journal of Clinical Nutrition, Cornell University, pg. 662, 2003

23. Agricultural Waste Management Field Handbook, US Department of Agriculture, Soil Conservation Service. USDA. p. 4 – 8, April 1992

24. Braxton Little, Jane. "The Ogallala Aquifer Saving a Vital US Water Source" *Scientific American*, March 30, 2009

25. John Vidal, "Scientists Warn of a World Forced into Vegetarianism" Climate Central, September 3, 2012,

26. Greg Lardy & Charles Stoltenow, "Livestock and Water" North Dakota State University and US Department of Agriculture, July 1999

27. "Sustainability of Meat-Based and Plant-Based Diets and the Environment" American Journal of Clinical Nutrition, Department of Ecology and Evolutionary Biology, Cornell University, pg. 662, 2003

28. A.Y. Hoekstra and A.K. Chapagain, "Water Footprints of Nations: Water Use By People As a Function of Their Consumptions Patterns," University of Twente, Enschede, The Netherlands, 2006

29. Robinson, Michelsen and Gollehon, "Mitigating water shortages in a multiple risk environment," Water Policy Vol 12 No 1, p. 114–128, 2010

30. "Profile of the Agricultural Livestock Production Industry" ,United States Enforcement and EPA, Environmental Protection Compliance Assurance, September 2000

31. Pimental, "Energy and Land Constraints in Food Protein Production," *Science Magazine*

32. "Risk Management Evaluation for Concentrated Animal Feeding Operations," US Environmental Protection Agency, EPA National Risk Management Laboratory, May 2004

33. McWilliams, James E., *Just Food*, Little, Brown & Co. copyright 2009, p.131

34. "What is Acid Rain?," US Environmental Protection Agency online, October 4, 2006

35. Thomas Harter, Harley Davis, Marsha C Mathews, Roland D Meyer, "Shallow groundwater quality on dairy farms with irrigated forage crops," Department of Land, Air, and Water Resources, University of California, Pages 287–315, April 2002

36. Burkholder, Libra, Weyer, Heathcote, Kolpin, Thorne, and Wichman, "Impacts of Waste from Concentrated Animal Feeding Operations on Water Quality," Environmental Health Perspectives, National Institute of Environmental Health Science, National Center for Biotechnology Information, February 2007

37. "Survey of the State of the World's Lakes," LEC/Lake Biwa Research Institute , International Lake Environment Committee, Otsu and United Nations Environment Programme

38. Rabalais, Eugene, Turner. Wiseman, Jr., "Gulf of Mexico Hypoxia, a.k.a. "The Dead Zone," Louisiana Universities Marine Consortium, Louisiana Coastal Ecology Institute, and Department of Oceanography & Coastal Sciences, Louisiana State University, pg. 236

39. Brian G. Henning, "Standing in Livestock's Long Shadow: The Ethics of Eating Meat on a Small Planet," Ethics & the Environment, Volume 16, Number 2, Fall 2011

40. Margulis & Sergio, "Causes of Deforestation of the Brazilian Amazon," The World Bank , 2004

41. "The Extinction Crisis," Center for Biological Diversity, http://www. biologicaldiversity.org/programs/biodiversity/elements_of_biodiversity/ extinction_crisis/index

42. H. Steinfeld et al, "Livestock's Long Shadow, Environmental Issues and Opinions," Food and Agriculture Organization of the United Nations, 2006

43. "Wildlife Damage Management" US Department of Agriculture, Wildlife Services' 2010 Program Data Reports

44. Pimentel and Pimentel, "Sustainability of Meat-Based and Plant- Based Diets and the Environment," Department of Ecology and Evolutionary Biology, Cornell University, *American Journal of Clinical Nutrition*, pg. 661, 662, 2003

45. "Invest In Agriculture For Food Security, The Whole World Will Profit," United Nations Food and Agriculture Organization, World Food Day, 2006

46. Oppenlander, Richard. author of *Comfortably Unaware,* lecture presented at the Conscious Eating Conference, UC Berkeley, February 2012

47. "Invest In Agriculture For Food Security, The Whole World Will Profit" United Nations Food and Agriculture Organization, World Food Day, 2006

48. Bralove, "The Food Crisis: the Shortages May Pit the 'Have Nots' Against the 'Haves'," Wall Street Journal

49. Philip Wollen, "Should Meat Be Off the Table?", Intelligence Squared Debate Series, National Public Radio

Chapter 6

1. Pierre Desrochers & Hiroko Shimizu, "Yes, We Have No Bananas: A Critic of the Food Miles Perspective," George Mason University, 2008

2. Christopher L. Weber & H. Scott Matthews, "Food-Miles and the Relative Climate Impacts of Food Choices in the United States" Department of Civil and Environmental Engineering and Department of Engineering and Public Policy, Carnegie Mellon University, April 16, 2008

3. Saunders, Caroline, Barber, Andrew, Taylor, Greg, "Food miles - comparative energy / emissions performance of New Zealand's agriculture industry" Lincoln University, Agribusiness and Economics Research Unit, July 2006

4. Christopher L. Weber and H. Scott Matthews, "Food-Miles and the Relative Climate Impacts of Food Choices in the United States" Department of Civil and Environmental Engineering and Department of Engineering and Public Policy, Carnegie Mellon University, April 16, 2008

5. H. Brunke, R. Howitt and D. Sumner, "Future Food Production and Consumption in California Under Alternative Scenarios" California Water Plan, Update Volume 4, University of California, Agricultural Issues Center, pg. 1, 6, 2005

6. J. Raloff, "Climate Friendly Dining...Meats, The Carbon Footprint of Raising Livestock for Food" *Science News*, February 15, 2009

7. Gidon Eshel, "Grass-fed beef packs a punch to environment" *Reuters*, April 8, 2010

8. McWilliams, James, "Fighting Cow Methane at the Source: Their Food" *Discover*, p.130, July 8, 2008

9. Jude Capper, "Is the Grass Always Greener? Comparing the Environmental Impact of Conventional, Natural and Grass-Fed Beef Production Systems" Department of Animal Sciences, Washington State University, April 10, 2012

10. McWilliams, James. *Just Food: Where Locavores Get it Wrong and How We Can truly Eat Responsibly*, Little, Brown & Co., June 9, 2010

11. H. Steinfeld et al, "Livestock's Long Shadow, Environmental Issues and Opinions" Food and Agriculture Organization of the United Nations, 2006

12. A. Rosati, A. Aumaitre, "Organic dairy farming in Europe" Livestock Production Science, Vol. 90, Issue 1, European Association for Animal Production, Pages 41–51, October 2004

13. Oppenlander, Richard. author of *Comfortably Unaware,* lecture presented at the Conscious Eating Conference, UC Berkeley, February 2012

14. Oppenlander, *ibid*

15. H. Steinfeld et al, "Livestock's Long Shadow, Environmental Issues and Opinions" Food and Agriculture Organization of the United Nations, pgs. 267, 273, 2006

16. Vasile Stanescu, "Green Eggs and Ham? The Myth of Sustainable Meat and the Danger of the Local" *The Journal of Critical Animal Studies,* VII. 3, 2009

17. "Rethinking Global Biodiversity Strategies: Exploring structural changes in production and consumption to reduce biodiversity loss" PBL Netherlands Environmental Assessment Agency, May 10, 2010

18. Elke Stehfest, Lex Bouwman, Detlef P. van Vuuren, Michel G. J. den Elzen, Bas Eickhout and Pavel Kabat, "Climate Benefits of Changing Diet," Netherlands Environmental Assessment Agency, Climatic Change, Volume 95, Issues 1–2, 2009

19. A.J. Belsky, A. Matzke, S. Uselman, "Survey of Livestock Influences on Stream and Riparian Ecosystems in the Western United States" *Journal of Soil and Water Conservation*, Vol. 54, pp. 419–431 pg. 429–31, 1999

20. Simon Eldridge, "Soil management for dairy and beef cattle grazing" NSW Agriculture, the Department of Infrastructure, Planning and Natural Resources, March 2004

21. McWilliams, James. "The Unequal Distribution of Waste" Eating Plants Blog, August 27, 2012

22. Oppenlander, Richard. author of *Comfortably Unaware,* lecture presented at the Conscious Eating Conference, UC Berkeley, February 2012

23. "Soy Benefits," National Soybean Research Laboratory, http://www.nsrl.uiuc.edu/soy_benefits.html

24. Karl-Ivar Kumm, "Sustainability of organic meat production under Swedish conditions" Department of Economics, Swedish University of Agricultural Sciences, Volume 88, Issue 1, January 2002

25. Imke J.M de Boer, "Environmental impact assessment of conventional and organic milk production" Animal Production Systems Group, Wageningen Institute of Animal Sciences, Volume 80, Issues 1–2, March 2003

26. "Organic: A Climate Savior? The foodwatch report on the greenhouse effect of conventional and organic farming in Germany" based on the study "The Impact of German Agriculture on the Climate," The Institute for Ecological Economy Research (IÖW) Deutsche Wildtier Stiftung, KLEF Karl Linder Education Foundation, 2007

Chapter 7

1. "Carcass Disposal: A Comprehensive Review" National Agricultural Biosecurity Center Consortium, USDA, APHIS Cooperative Agreement Project, Carcass Disposal Working Group, pg. 9, August 2004

2. W Morgan Morrow and Peter R Ferket, "The Disposal of Dead Pigs, A Review" Swine Health and Production, Vol. 1, p.1 May, 1993

3. "The Environmental Impact of the Animal Product Processing Industries" United Nations, Food and Agriculture Organization

4. "BSE (Bovine Spongiform Encephalopathy, or Mad Cow Disease)" Center for Disease Control and Prevention (CDC), National Center for Emerging and Zoonotic Infectious Diseases (NCEZID), Division of High-Consequence Pathogens and Pathology, September 14, 2012

5. Kristian Foden-Vencil, "Rendering Crisis Hits Oregon Livestock Industry" Oregon Public Broadcasting Online, October 20, 2008

6. "Carcass Disposal: A Comprehensive Review" National Agricultural Biosecurity Center Consortium, USDA APHIS Cooperative Agreement Project, Carcass Disposal Working Group, Chapter 1, pg. 8, 9, August 2004

7. "Carcass Disposal: A Comprehensive Review" National Agricultural Biosecurity Center Consortium, USDA APHIS Cooperative Agreement

Project, Carcass Disposal Working Group, Chapter 1, pg. 6, August 2004

8. W Morgan Morrow and Peter R Ferket, "The Disposal of Dead Pigs, A Review" Swine Health and Production, Vol. 1, p.1, 2

9. "Carcass Disposal: A Comprehensive Review" National Agricultural Biosecurity Center Consortium, USDA APHIS Cooperative Agreement Project, Carcass Disposal Working Group, Chapter 1, pg. 7, August 2004

10. Shui-Jen Chen, Ming-Cheng Hung, Kuo-Lin Huang, Wen-Ing Hwang, "Emission of heavy metals from animal carcass incinerators in Taiwan" Department of Environmental Engineering and Science, National Pingtung University of Science and Technology, June 2004

11. "Carcass Disposal: A Comprehensive Review" National Agricultural Biosecurity Center Consortium, USDA APHIS Cooperative Agreement Project, Carcass Disposal Working Group, Chapter 1, pg. 15 August 2004

Chapter 8

1. B. Worm, *et al*, "Impacts of Biodiversity Loss on Ocean Ecosystem Services" *Science Magazine* 314, 787–79, 2006

2. "Turning the Tide on Falling Fish Stocks" United Nations Environment Programme, UNEP-Led Green Economy Charts Sustainable Investment Path, May 17, 2010

3. Nash, Madeleine, "The fish crisis: the oceans that once seemed a bottomless source of high-protein, low-fat food are rapidly being depleted" *The New York Times, Time Magazine,* August 1997

4. Nash, Madeleine, "The fish crisis: the oceans that once seemed a bottomless source of high-protein, low-fat food are rapidly being depleted" *The New York Times, Time Magazine,* August 1997

5. Cetacean Bycatch Resource Center, www.cetaceanbycatch.org, Accessed May 25, 2010.

6. The Consortium for Wildlife Bycatch Reduction, New England Aquarium, www.neaq.org

7. Harrington, Myers, Rosenberg, "Wasted Fishery Resources: Discarded By-Catch in the USA" 2Biology Department, Dalhousie University, Ocean Process and Analysis Laboratory, Institute for the Study of Earth, Oceans and Space, University of New Hampshire, 2005

8. Dr. J. Talberth, K. Wolowicz et al, "The Ecological Fishprint of Nations: Measuring Humanity's Impact on Marine Ecosystems" University of British Columbia, The Ocean Project, Center for Sustainable Economy, Redefining Progress, 2006

9. Owen, James, "Nets Kill Nearly 1,000 Marine Mammals a Day, Group Says," *National Geographic News*, June 10, 2005

10. "World Wildlife Fund Position on Whaling and the IWC" Whales, Whaling and the International Whaling Commission, World Wildlife Fund International, , p. 2, May, 2007

11. The Consortium for Wildlife Bycatch Reduction, New England Aquarium, www.neaq.org

12. Costal Conservation Association, Bluefin Tuna Campaign, http://www.joincca.org/issues/8

13. S. Holt, "The Food Resources of the Ocean," *Scientific American*, 221:178–194.

14. "Fish Guts Explain Marine Carbon Cycle Mystery," University of Exeter, *ScienceDaily*. June 1, 2011

15. "The Surprising Sources of Your Favorite Seafoods" National Oceanic and Atmospheric Administration, NOAA, website, Fisheries Service, October 2012

16. "Impacts of Freshwater and Marine Aquaculture on the Environment: Knowledge and Gaps" EVS Environmental Consultants, June 2000

17. Brian Halweil and Danielle Nierenberg, "Meat and Seafood: The Global Diet's Most Costly Ingredients" 2008 State of the World, *World Watch Institute*, p. 6

18. Thurston Clarke, "Sea of Troubles" *New York Times*, citing the book: *The Empty Ocean, Plundering the World's Marine Life*, May 25, 2003

19. "The Surprising Sources of Your Favorite Seafoods" National Oceanic and Atmospheric Administration, NOAA, website, Fisheries Service, October 2012

20. Steven E. Campana, Josh Brading, and Warren Joyce, "Estimation of Pelagic Shark Bycatch and Associated Mortality in Canadian Atlantic Fisheries" Canadian Science Advisory Secretariat, Research Document 2011/067, Fisheries and Oceans Canada, 2011

21. "Caught in the Trade" Conservation International website, www.conservation.org

22. Calum Brown, Keven Laland, Jens Krause, "Fish Cognition and Behavior" *Journal Fish and Fisheries*, Nov. 20, 2007

23. Nordgreen et al, "Thermonociception in fish: Effects of two different doses of morphine on thermal threshold and post-test behavior in goldfish (Carassius auratus)" Applied Animal Behavior Science, 2009

24. Sneddon L.U., Braithwaite V.A. & Gentle M.J., "Do fish have nociceptors: Evidence for the evolution of a vertebrate sensory system" 2003

25. Rose, J., "The Neurobehavioral Nature of Fishes and the Question of Awareness and Pain" Reviews in *Fisheries Science*, 101–38, 2003

26. Leake, Jonathan , "Anglers to Face RSPCA Checks" *Times Online*. March 14, 2004

27. Braithwaite, Victoria. *Do Fish Feel Pain?*, Oxford University Press, 2010

28. Stuart Barr, Peter R. Laming, Jaimie T.A. Dick, Robert W. Elwood, "Nociception or pain in a decapod crustacean?" School of Biological Sciences, Queen's University Belfast, U.K., Volume 75, Issue 3, March 2008

29. R. Elwood, M. Appel, "Pain experience in hermit crabs" School of Biological Sciences, Queen's University, U.K. Volume 77, Issue 5, May 2009

30. R. Elwood, S. Barr, L. Patterson, "Pain and stress in crustaceans?" School of Biological Sciences, Queen's University, Volume 118, Issues 3–4, May 2009

31. "Final Report: Evaluation of Procedures to Reduce Delayed Mortality of Black Bass Following Summer Tournaments" Oklahoma Department of Wildlife Conservation. Federal Aid Grant No. F-50-R, Fish Research for Oklahoma Waters, Project No. 8, February 28, 1997

32. "The Madison Declaration on Mercury Pollution," A Journal of the Human Environment: Vol. 36, No. 1, pgs. 62–66

33. L.R. Bordajandi, G.Gómez, M.A. Fernández, E. Abad, J. Rivera, M.J. González, Chemosphere, "Study on PCBs, PCDD/Fs, organochlorine pesticides, heavy metals and arsenic content in freshwater fish species from the River Turia (Spain)" Volume 53, Issue 2, Pages 163–171, October 2003

34. Andrew E. Smith, SM, ScD, State Toxicologist, Eric Frohmberg, MA, Toxicologist, "Evaluation of the Health Implications of Levels of Polychlorinated Dibenzo-p-Dioxins (dioxins) and Polychlorinated Dibenzofurans (furans) in Fish from Maine Rivers" Environmental and Occupational Health Programs, Maine Center for Disease Control, Maine Department of Health and Human Services, January 2008

Chapter 9

1. US Census Bureau, International Data Base, June 2011, http://www.census.gov/population/international/data/idb/worldpopgraph.php

2. Hanna L. Tuomisto, M. Joost Teixeira de Mattos, "Environmental Impacts of Cultured Meat Production" University of Oxford, Wildlife Conservation Research Unit, June 17, 2011

3. *ibid*

4. New Harvest Website, www.new-harvest.org

Chapter 10

1. Academy of Nutrition and Dietetics Website, Vegetarian Lifestyle, 2012 http://www.eatright.org/Public/content.aspx?id=6372

2. "ACS Guidelines on Nutrition and Physical Activity for Cancer Prevention" American Cancer Society, January 2012

3. "Fortify Your Health With a Nutritious Diet," American Heart Association, American Diabetes Association, American Cancer Society, http://www.everydaychoices.org/eat.html

4. "Healthy Eating for Older Adults, Nutrition for Kids & Teens," American Dietetic Association, Academy of Nutrition and Dietetics

5. ACS Guidelines on Nutrition and Physical Activity for Cancer Prevention," American Cancer Society, January 2012

6. American Heart Association Website, Grocery Shopping, Vegetables and Fruits, puts significant restrictions on meat consumption and even recommends to, "Select more meat substitutes such as dried beans, peas, lentils or tofu (soybean curd) and use them as entrees or in salads and soups."

7. In a letter from Timothy J. Gardner, President of the American Heart Association to the USDA and the Department of Health and Human Services, Dr. Gardner recommends that, "The recommendations should also emphasize nonanimal-based sources of protein such as legumes and beans. Consumption of plant-based sources of protein may facilitate the displacement of other foods from the diet such as fatty meats." January 2009 http://www.heart.org/idc/groups/heart-public/@wcm/@ adv/documents/downloadable/ucm_312853.pdf

8. Francesco Visioli, Luisa Borsani, Claudio Galli, "European Society for Cardiology, Diet and Prevention of Coronary Heart Disease: The Potential role of Phytochemicals" Oxford Journals, Cardiovascular Research, 2000

9. "The Basics of the Nutritional Facts Panel" American Dietetic Association, Academy of Nutrition and Dietetics

10. "Vegetarian Diets" Academy of Nutrition and Dietetics, Volume 109, Issue 7, Pages 1266–1282, July 2009

11. Choose My Plate, US Department of Agriculture, http://www. choosemyplate.gov/

12. "Vegetarianism, Mortality and Metabolic Risk: The New Adventist Health Study" Report presented at Academy of Nutrition and Dietetic (Food and Nutrition Conference) Annual Meeting; October 7, 2012

13. Freston, Kathy, "Why Do Vegetarians Live Longer?" *The Huffington Post*, October 26, 2012 cited: "Risk factors for mortality in the nurses' health study: a competing risks analysis." Baer HJ, et al, 173(3):319–29, February 2011

14. Tantamango-Bartley Y, Jaceldo-Siegl K, Fan J, Fraser G., "Vegetarian diets and the incidence of cancer in a low-risk population" Cancer Epidemiological Biomarkers, Nov 20, 2012

15. J. David Spence, David J.A. Jenkins, Jean Davignon, "Egg yolk consumption and carotid plaque" Atherosclerosis, Volume 224, Issue 2 , Pages 469–473, July 18, 2012

16. Richman, Kenfield, Stampfer, Giovannucci, and Chan, "Egg, red meat, and poultry intake and risk of lethal prostate cancer in the prostate specific antigen-era: incidence and survival" American Association for Cancer Research, September 9, 2011

17. Richard R Rosenkranz, Sara K Rosenkranz and Kelly JJ Neessen, "Dietary factors associated with lifetime asthma or hayfever diagnosis in Australian middle-aged and older adults: a cross-sectional study" Nutrition Journal 2012, 11:84, October 2012

18. Dr. Michael Greger, "Heart Disease," NutritionFacts.org, http://nutritionfacts.org/topics/heart-disease/ *and* Dr. Michael Greger, "Cancer," NutritionFacts.org, http://nutritionfacts.org/topics/cancer/

19. "How safe is that chicken? Most tested broilers were contaminated," *Consumer Reports Magazine*, January 2010

20. Hardy TA, Blum S, McCombe PA, Reddel SW, "Guillain-barré syndrome: modern theories of etiology" Curr Allergy Asthma Rep., June 2011

Tam CC, Rodrigues LC, Petersen I, Islam A, Hayward A, O'Brien SJ, "Incidence of Guillain-Barré syndrome among patients with Campylobacter infection: a general practice research database study" J Infect Dis., July 2006

Nachamkin I, Allos BM, Ho T, "Campylobacter species and Guillain-Barré syndrome" Clin Microbiol Rev. July 11, 1998.

21. Rusin P, Orosz-Coughlin P, Gerba C., "Reduction of fecal coliform, coliform and heterotrophic plate count bacteria in the household kitchen and bathroom by disinfection with hypochlorite cleaners" Department of Soil, Water and Environmental Science, University of Arizona, November 1998

22. "What's in that pork? We found antibiotic-resistant bacteria and traces of a veterinary drug" *Consumer Reports magazine*, January 2013

23. "Dioxins and their effects on human health" World Health Organization, Fact sheet N°225, May 2010

24. "CDC research shows outbreaks linked to imported foods increasing" Center for Disease Control and Prevention, press release, March 14, 2012

25. "Center for Disease Control and Prevention, *Klebsiella* pneumoniae in Healthcare Settings" National Center for Emerging and Zoonotic Infectious Diseases (NCEZID), Division of Healthcare Quality Promotion (DHQP), August 27, 2012

26. Mohamed Nawaz, S.A. Khan, Q. Tran, K. Sung, A.A. Khan, I. Adamu, R.S. Steele, "Isolation and characterization of multidrug-resistant *Klebsiella* spp. isolated from shrimp imported from Thailand" Division of Microbiology, National Center for Toxicological Research, US Food and Drug Administration, International Journal of Food Microbiology, Pages 179–184, April 2012

27. Dr. Michael Greger, www.nutritionfacts.org

28. T. Colin Campbell Foundation, www.tcolincampbell.org

29. Dr. Neal Barnard, Physicians Committee for Responsible Medicine (PCRM), www.nealbarnard.org

30. Jack Norris RD, www.jacknorrisrd.com

Chapter 11

1. Nathan Wolfe, virologist, professor of epidemiology at UCLA and author of *The Viral Storm, The Dawn of a New Pandemic Age,* interview on National Public Radio, October 12, 2012

2. Nugent, Tom. "Preventing the Next Plague" *Stanford Magazine,* March/ April 2007

3. Nathan Wolfe, virologist, professor of epidemiology at UCLA and author of *The Viral Storm, The Dawn of a New Pandemic Age,* interview on National Public Radio, October 12, 2012

4. "Updated CDC Estimates of 2009 H1N1 Influenza Cases, Hospitalizations and Deaths in the United States, April 2009 – April 10, 2010" Center for Disease Control and Prevention

5. Nathan Wolfe, virologist, professor of epidemiology at UCLA and author of *The Viral Storm, The Dawn of a New Pandemic Age,* interview on National Public Radio, October 12, 2012

6. "Evolution of Staph 'Superbug' Traced Between Humans and Livestock" Science Daily, February 21, 2011

7. "Livestock Boom Risks Aggravating Animal "Plagues," Poses Threat to Food Security and World's Poor" Science Daily, February 11, 2011

8. A. Kijlstra, I.A.J.M. Eijck, "Animal health in organic livestock production systems: a review" NJAS - Wageningen Journal of Life Sciences, Volume 54, Issue 1, Pages 77–94, 2006

9. Mette Vaarst, Susanne Padel, Malla Hovi, David Younie, Albert Sundrum, "Sustaining animal health and food safety in European organic livestock farming" Livestock Production Science, Volume 94, Issues 1–2, Pages 61–69, June 2005

10. "Animal health in organic livestock production systems: a review" University Wageningen & Res Ctr, Animal Science Group, NL-1200 AB Lelystad, Netherlands, March 2006

11. Dubey, Hill, Rozeboom, Rajendran, Choudhary, Ferreira, Kwok, Su, "High prevalence and genotypes of Toxoplasma gondii isolated from

organic pigs in northern USA" Veterinary Parasitology, Volume 188, Issues 1–2, 13 Pages 14–18, August 2012

12. "Food Safety in Free-Range and Organic Livestock Systems: Risk Management and Responsibility" Journal of Food Protection, Vol. 72, No. 12, Pages 2629–2637, 2009

13. Astrid M., Anja R. Heckeroth, and Louis M. Weiss, "Toxoplasma gondii: From Animals to Humans" Tenter National Institute of Heath, US National Library of Medicine, Nov. 30, 2000

14. "Dioxins and their effects on human health" World Health Organization, Fact sheet N°225, May 2010

15. "Bacterial resistance to antibiotics: a means of monitoring organic pork production?" Agriculture; Food Science & Technology; Toxicology (provided by Thomson Reuters), Universidad de Santiago de Compostela, Lugo, Spain, March 2000

16. Peter R. Davies, "Intensive Swine Production and Pork Safety, Foodborne Pathogens and Disease" 8(2): 189–201, February 2011

17. Davies. *Ibid.*

18. Davies. *Ibid.*

19. McWilliams, James. "The Meat Myth: Free-Range isn't Always Safer," *The Atlantic,* June 1, 2011

20. Dahl, Permin, Christensen, Bisgaard, Muhairwa, Petersen, Poulsen, Jensen, "The effect of concurrent infections with Pasteurella multocida and Ascaridia galli on free range chickens" Veterinary microbiology 86. 4, pp. 313–324, May 24, 2002

21. Overmeire, I van; Pussemier, L; Hanot, V; Temmerman, L de; Hoenig, M; Goeyens, L, "Chemical contamination of free-range eggs from Belgium" Food additives and contaminants, 2006

22. Hsu, Jing-Fang; Chen, Chun; Liao, Pao-Chi, "Elevated PCDD/F Levels and Distinctive PCDD/F Congener Profiles in Free Range Eggs" Journal of agricultural and food chemistry, Jul 14, 2010

23. Oddvar Fossum, Désirée S. Jansson, Pernille Engelsen Etterlin and Ivar Vågsholm, "Causes of Mortality in Laying Hens in Different Housing Systems in 2001 to 2004" Department of Animal Health and Antimicrobial Strategies, National Veterinary Institute (SVA), National Veterinary Institute, Uppsala, Sweden

24. Bailey, J.S.; Cosby, D.E., "Salmonella Prevalence in Free-Range and Certified Organic Chicken" Journal of Food Protection®, Volume 68, Number 11, November 2005

25. Rothschid, Mary. "39 Ill From Salmonella Tainted Chicks, Ducklings" *Food Safety News*, June 10, 2011

26. Gaffga, NH, *et al*, "Outbreak of Salmonellosis Linked to Live Poultry from a Mail-Order Hatchery" New England Journal of Medicine, Center for Disease Control & Prevention, May 31, 2012

27. Devon Fredericksen, "Take Care to Avoid Risk with Backyard Chickens *Food Safety News*, June 13, 2011,

28. "What is Salmonellosis?" Center For Disease Control and Prevention, April 5, 2012

29. Van Loo, et al, *The Future of Organic Meats, in Organic Meat Production and Processing* published by John Wiley and Sons, Oxford, UK. Copyright 2012, Institute for Food and Technologies

30. Crystal Smith-Spangler, MD, MS; et al, "Are Organic Foods Safer or Healthier than Conventional Alternatives? A Systematic Review" Annals of Internal Medicine, 2012

Chapter 12

1. "How Many Adults are Vegan in the US?" The Vegetarian Resource Group, December 5, 2011

2. Hopkins, Katy. "Colleges That Offer Courses, Choices for Vegetarians," USNews.com, Education, June 7, 2011

3. Runkle, Nathan. "Veg*nism a Growing Trend among College Students," Mercy for Animals, The MFA Blog, October 15, 2010

4. United Egg Producers, General US Statistics, Egg Industry Fact Sheet, June, 2012

5. "Poultry Slaughter 2011 Summery" USDA, National Agricultural Statistics Service, February 2012

6. Steve Meyer and Len Steiner, "Daily Livestock Report," GME Group, Vol. 9, No. 22, February 2, 2011

7. Jurek, Scott. "Ultramarathon Running: How A Vegan Diet Helped Me Run 100 Miles," *Huffington Post,* June 12, 2012

8. "Build Muscle, No Steak Required" Academy of Nutrition and Dietetics, http://www.eatright.org/

9. For an extensive list of vegan bodybuilders and their profiles please visit the Vegan Bodybuilding and Fitness website created by Robert Cheeke: http://veganbodybuilding.com/?page=bios

10. Visit the Veganic Agriculture Network site: http://www.goveganic.net/